The Politics
of Welfare

BLANCHE BERNSTEIN

The Politics
of Welfare
The New York City
Experience

Abt Books
Cambridge, Massachusetts

Library of Congress Cataloging in Publication Data

Bernstein, Blanche, 1912–
　The politics of welfare.

　Bibliography.
　Includes index.
　1. Public welfare—New York (N.Y.)—Case studies.
2. United States—Social policy.　I. Title.
HV99.N59B44 1982　　　361.6'09747'1　　　82-6863
ISBN 0-89011-570-2　　　　　　　　　　　　AACR2

Printed in the United States of America

Design by Marianne Rubenstein

ISBN: 0-89011-570-2

TO MY BROTHER
HILLIARD L. BERNSTEIN
who so often has been so helpful

CONTENTS

ACKNOWLEDGMENTS

This book could not have been written without the aid of a great many people.

I am most grateful for financial support from the Ford Foundation, the Institute for Educational Affairs, the Lehrman Institute, and the Social Research Institute of the New School for Social Research, and for unfailing moral support from Henry Cohen, Dean, Graduate School of Management and Urban Professions at the New School.

There are many former colleagues in New York City's Human Resources Administration and the New York State Department of Social Services whose knowledge and goodwill I exploited, often outrageously. Among those in HRA are Herb Rosenzweig, former Deputy Administrator for Income Maintenance, Martin Burdick, formerly Assistant Deputy and now acting Deputy Administrator for Income Maintenance, and Irwin I. Brooks, Assistant Commissioner for the Office of Income Support. They amassed for me from their files a huge number of letters, memoranda, and other unpublished documents relevant to the subjects covered in this book. They also read and commented on drafts of the chapters dealing with public assistance and work programs, food stamps, and the child support program. At NYSDSS, Sydelle Shapiro, Deputy Commissioner for

Income Maintenance, John Harwick, Director of the Food Stamp Program, and Meldon F. Kelsey, Director of the Office of Child Support Enforcement, were most helpful in providing me with necessary documents and comments on drafts of the chapters on food stamps and child support, and Jack Hickey, Assistant Commissioner, Division of Income Maintenance, was, as always, available and able to answer a question or clarify a regulation.

Robert J. Fersh, formerly confidential assistant to the Administrator, Food and Nutrition Service, U.S. Department of Agriculture, graciously responded to my request for copies of unpublished documents from welfare administrators in various states, particularly their comments on USDA's draft regulations implementing the 1977 food stamp amendments, and for his comments on the draft chapter.

The Lehrman Institute, as is its custom, formed a study group of highly knowledgeable people to review and discuss with the author drafts of each of the chapters. I benefited greatly from their observations in the course of three meetings and am most grateful to them for taking time out of their busy schedules for this task.

Three young graduate students worked with me at different times plowing through piles of published and unpublished documents, and preparing notes and summaries. They are Andrew Paparozzi, Columbia University, Judith Lilleston, Graduate Center, City University, and Mark Wasserman, Graduate School of Management and Urban Professions, New School. I appreciate their assistance.

Hildred Brown, my secretary, patiently and diligently typed and retyped the many drafts, never complaining and frequently encouraging me by saying she found the text interesting.

I have indeed had a great deal of help from many people, including many I have not named. If any errors remain in the text, only I am to blame.

Blanche Bernstein
New York City
January 1982

CHAPTER 1

Introduction

Many early nineteenth-century novels open with the hero (or heroine) explaining who he is, where he was born, and how he came to write the tale he is about to tell. This book is not a novel, but it is an account, based in part on my personal experience as a welfare analyst and administrator, of how and why welfare programs developed and expanded in unanticipated ways and with unanticipated and often deleterious effects. It seems appropriate, therefore, to begin by explaining why and how I became involved in welfare administration, what my general approach to social welfare programs is, and why this book might be of interest.

During much of the 1950s, my professional efforts were directed to research focused on the growth and characteristics of the population of New York City and the social problems of the vulnerable groups in the city—children, youth, the aged. In the 1960s, my interest shifted to social development on the international scene, with emphasis on the developing countries. Nevertheless, as a devoted New Yorker, I continued to follow events in the city, and my curiosity was aroused by a newspaper story indicating that the welfare caseload in New York City

1

had doubled between 1961 and 1967. Population trends did not explain it. Migration from Puerto Rico and the South had substantially fallen off from the high levels of the fifties.* Locally, as well as nationally, unemployment was down from what had been considered the very high level of 6 percent in 1961 to 4 percent; it was to drop in 1969 to what is now regarded as the unachievably low rate of 3 percent—and real wages were rising.

Clearly, neither population trends nor the economic situation explained the doubling of the caseload. What was the reason, then? When I returned to New York City from Washington D.C. in 1969 and again turned to research, I began to study the public assistance program. In the course of the following seven years, I completed a series of studies which pointed up what in my judgment were serious flaws in the administration or management of the program and unanticipated adverse effects of legislative and administrative policies.

My studies led me to five major conclusions: (1) the number of persons on welfare who were in fact not eligible to receive it appeared to be far higher than welfare officials were admitting; (2) the size of the welfare package, when one took into account cash grants for the basic allowance and rent, food stamps, school lunches, and medical assistance, was far larger than had been realized; (3) the value of the welfare package translated into its gross income equivalent, while it did not provide a luxurious level of living, was substantial enough to constitute a disincentive to work at unskilled or semiskilled jobs; (4) the availability of substantial welfare benefits had an adverse impact on family stability; and (5) the formation and continuation of the intact family (father, mother, and children) was the most important single factor in preventing dependency.

These findings challenged the conventional rhetoric, conventionally regarded as liberal, of many welfare officials, social

---

*While it is not true that people migrate to New York in order to go on welfare, recent migrants or immigrants are a vulnerable group more likely to need welfare when they lose a job or some catastrophe strikes than those who have been in the city longer and are better established.

welfare organizations, welfare advocacy groups, and minority leaders in New York and throughout the country, and they were not welcomed by these groups. Throughout the 1960s and until 1973, New York City welfare commissioners and their deputies insisted that ineligibility was no higher than the tolerable level of 3 percent—at most, 6 percent. It turned out, in fact, to be over 18 percent. In decrying the inadequacy of the welfare standard, critics rarely made reference to in-kind benefits such as food stamps or medical assistance. Certainly, the notion of translating the welfare package into its gross income equivalent had never been entertained; indeed, many welfare community leaders regarded such a notion as anathema.*

In response to evidence that the welfare package had an adverse impact on incentives to work, many welfare officials at first simply denied the existence of any problem, asserting that welfare clients preferred to work and would take jobs if they were available. Their position evolved, however, and subsequently they espoused the view that one could not expect welfare clients to work if they ended up with only slightly more net income than was available from welfare. As a result, these officials promoted welfare reforms which would ensure a sufficiently large differential between net income from work and the welfare grant to make working "worthwhile."

Perhaps most revealing was the lack of interest on the part of many welfare officials, and much of the organized social welfare community in general, in confronting the problem of family break-up—indeed, in recognizing it as a major cause of welfare dependency. These groups preferred to ascribe dependency to racial discrimination, unemployment levels, inadequate schools, inadequate housing, or the unjust distribution of income in a capitalist society—explanations which justified their refusal to

---

*A colleague told me of his discussion with one former New York City deputy commissioner who said, "If Blanche is right, we are all in trouble." A former commissioner asked a major research institute to undertake a study to disprove my findings; the study was undertaken but ended up basically supporting my conclusions.

undertake the admittedly difficult task of finding ways to reverse the trend toward family break-up.

The sixties were a time of turbulence, of mounting concern over the continued existence of poverty in America and an increasing sense of guilt over evidence of the sorry effects of past discrimination, as well as the level of continuing discrimination against blacks and Hispanics. The period was characterized by dismay at the denial of civil rights in some areas of the country, or the denial of some civil rights in all areas, and by anxiety about the violent reaction, reflected in the riots in many cities, to what were perceived as past and current injustices. In this atmosphere, a coalition developed, made up of the organized social welfare community in New York and other cities, many black and Hispanic leaders, the liberals, ill-defined as the term may be, and some of the liberal or radical clergy. This coalition looked to the welfare system as a major vehicle for righting the injustices of the society. The tripling of the caseload in New York City from 1961 to 1969, its quadrupling by 1972, and a comparable expansion throughout the country were less a cause of concern over the evidence of increasing dependency than a cause for rejoicing that justice was finally being done.

Under both Democratic and Republican administrations in Washington and at the state level, the coalition effectively promoted legislation and implemented regulations which made welfare an attractive option. The obligations of the head of the family to support the family were diminished, the welfare client was offered the choice of welfare instead of work, and—to enhance the dignity of welfare clients—the system was administered so loosely, as to permit widespread fraud and abuse. It was a perversion of the liberal ideal, which sought a greater equality of income distribution and the elimination of poverty through education and training, equal opportunity, and increased earnings from work and which looked to adequate welfare programs to care for those with no other alternative.

The judiciary helped in this process by its insistence on so closely guarding the rights of the client as to distort legislative intent and hamstring effective administration. Prodded by the newly developed public interest law firms, the judiciary displayed a degree of activism previously unknown, injecting itself into issues normally the sole province of legislative bodies or of the executive organ of government.

What was overlooked or ignored by those rejoicing in or complacent about the vastly increased welfare caseload was the enormous growth during the sixties and continuing through the seventies of female-headed families as a result of family breakup or the nonformation of families; this phenomenon, particularly marked in the black and Hispanic communities, was what led to the quadrupling of the welfare caseload in New York and most of the major cities in the country. One may quarrel over the question whether the availability of welfare was in part responsible for this trend.[1] One cannot, however, quarrel about the degree of social pathology which is found among female-headed families on welfare. In New York City, half of the school dropouts, half of the juvenile delinquents, and half of the young drug users were from families receiving Aid to Families with Dependent Children (AFDC)—a disproportionate share, by far.[2]

Nor can one dispute the close relationship between the female-headed family and poverty. Dr. Robert Hill of the National Urban League writes, "While the number of poor white families declined by two percent . . . between 1969 and 1978, the number of poor Black families rose by 19 percent . . . Because of the sharp rise in the number of Black families headed by women, they accounted *for all of the increase in the number of poor Black families over the decade.* While the number of poor Black families headed by men fell by 34 percent—between 1969 and 1978, the number of poor Black families headed by women soared by 64 percent" *(italics added)*.[3]

The net result of the huge increase in welfare caseloads was that by the end of the sixties there was general agreement among liberals, moderates, and conservatives that welfare was a mess, but little agreement as to why it was or what should be done about it. I have for some years had serious doubts that the panacea for the "welfare mess" or the elimination of poverty lay in welfare reform in the sense of President Richard Nixon's Family

Assistance Plan or President Jimmy Carter's Better Jobs and Income or other varieties of the negative income tax. I do not believe that a reduction in dependency or poverty will be achieved by just the right formula of benefit level and marginal tax rates. Rather, it is my view that with all its complexities, some of which could be reduced by less than drastic policy changes at the federal and state levels, the welfare system can be administered effectively, efficiently, and compassionately for those who need cash assistance for a short or long period and that it can be administered in a way that reduces dependency, to some degree. Achievement of the goal of a major reduction in dependency, however, depends on appropriate economic policies and a reduction in family instability.

The effectiveness of a welfare program is, in the first instance, a matter of appropriate legislative policies. But of equal importance is the way these policies are reflected in regulations issued at the federal or state levels and in how they are administered or managed at the local level. There is a surprisingly wide range of choices to be made.

In the vast literature on welfare, relatively little attention has been paid to the role of the nitty-gritty of administration in determining the effectiveness of the program. To quote one welfare analyst who did recognize its importance: "Administration is perhaps the most unexciting, intractable area in which to initiate welfare reform. People's eyes glaze over at the first mention of reorganization, revised regulations, and improved personnel administration. But dull as the area may be to most, it is of critical importance in any effective welfare reform plan."[4] Further, insufficient attention has been given to the impact on the quality of administration of the values and attitudes of those who manage the program and those who influence them, the political constituency for welfare.

How policy goals and issues are defined and how the goals of administration are determined and implemented depend on the values—or the politics—of a large and varied cast of characters: the President, governors, mayors, and other elected officials and legislators, as well as appointed officials at the federal and state levels, individual welfare administrators, the courts, labor unions, ethnic and religious groups, the organized social welfare community, and welfare advocacy and local community groups. How elected and appointed officials gauge the importance of special interest groups and how the pressures they exert affect the officials' perception of the underlying consensus of the general population (or those of the general population who vote) will influence enormously, if not determine, policy, regulation, and management.

Perhaps the most important single action a governor or mayor takes in relation to welfare policy and management is the appointment of the head of the state or city social welfare agency. For while one should not minimize the difficulties of changing the inner life of a bureaucracy, the commissioner's views, values, and approaches to social welfare problems will have a significant impact on the direction set for the agency, on the determination of its priorities, and, of paramount importance, on the appointment of top staff who, in turn, will determine the effectiveness of management and the quality of service to clients. Equally important, the person chosen as commissioner is likely to be one who reflects the governor's or mayor's values and responses to the pressures of special interest groups. My own experience as an appointed official is illustrative of the impact of special interest groups, or of the politics of welfare.

Hugh Carey, who took office as governor of New York in January 1975, announced in his inaugural message that the days of wine and roses were over. State finances were strained, and the fiscal crisis in New York City was to erupt publicly in only a few months. The time had come for some accelerated efforts to control the ever-mounting costs of public assistance, Medicaid, and other social welfare programs in the state and in New York City. Stephen Berger was appointed state Commissioner of Social Services in May 1975, and he subsequently appointed me Deputy Commissioner for Income Maintenance. It represented a decision on his part, and, I assume, on the governor's, to brave the anticipated criticism from the social welfare community at the appointment of a "hard-liner." Criticism there was, but rather muted, certainly compared with what was to happen later.

During the two years or so of my tenure, a major focus of my efforts was improving the integrity of the public assistance program throughout the state, but particularly in New York City, where 60 percent of the state's welfare caseload resided and where the problem was most acute. Substantial progress was achieved despite some initial resistance from city welfare officials and despite their continuing reluctance to give a high priority to reducing ineligibility and over- or underpayment to welfare clients.

Subsequently, after Edward Koch was elected mayor, he appointed me administrator of New York City's Human Resources Administration (HRA), recognizing that the appointment would not be received with universal acclaim.* A *New York Times* editorial on January 6, 1978, said that "to direct the Human Resources Administration, Mayor Koch has dared to select an acerbic, unsentimental, highly schooled critic of governmental welfare policies." In general, the major newspapers supported my appointment, but not the *Amsterdam News*. Andy Cooper, in his column "One Man's Opinion" on January 5, said, "The Bernstein appointment has raised eyebrows . . . because of her reputation of being 'anti-poor' " and called for "black

---

*The background to this appointment is of some relevance. I had earlier been appointed by then mayor-elect Koch as co-chair of the search committee that was to make recommendations about an administrator for HRA. But, after considering the search committee's recommendations, Koch asked me to become administrator of HRA, even though I advised him that my appointment would not be popular with the social welfare community. We both underestimated the reaction, especially of the black leaders. In the light of subsequent events, I should note that the first time I ever met mayor-elect Koch was when I was introduced to him at a meeting of the chairpersons of all the search committees. His unforgettable remark was, "How d'ya do?" Despite some notions to the contrary, my political connections are nil, and the extent of my political party commitment is that I am enrolled in the Democratic party.

leaders to insist on her immediate removal."* Over the next year, the attacks from black leaders continued and mounted in intensity. I was also having problems with the mostly white social welfare community. Aside from their lack of enthusiasm for what they regarded as my undue concern with ineligibility, part of the difficulty stemmed from a difference of opinion about the role of the commissioner; part involved appointments of blacks to top positions; and part involved policy decisions.

The social welfare community in New York City includes the directors and staff of voluntary social agencies and, to some extent, their lay boards, coordinating groups such as the Community Council of Greater New York, deans and faculty of schools of social work, and the social work profession in general. It has long regarded the commissioner of HRA as one of its own, who should be mainly an advocate for the poor. I regarded myself as a concerned public servant with the responsibility for administering social welfare programs for the poor and vulnerable population of the city within the framework of the laws and regulations, and within the fiscal realities constraining the state and city.

This difference in our views on the commissioner's role led to different approaches to specific issues. For example, early in the 1978 state legislative session, the black caucus, under the leadership of then Senator Carl McCall, urged an increase in the basic welfare grant, a position supported by many of the social welfare organizations. At this time, neither the state nor the city administration could give priority to such an increase in expenditures. The city was still three years away from a balanced budget, and the state was hard pressed to maintain a precarious balance. In this situation, I did not express support of the proposal. Indeed, I would have regarded my support as the result

---

*My summary response to a reporter doing a special story about me was, "I'm anti-poor in only one sense. I would like to help the poor break out of poverty and get into the middle-class as soon as possible" (*New York Post,* January 18, 1978).

of a cynical arrangement to permit the commissioner to gather the plaudits of the social welfare community while the mayor saw to the legislative defeat of the proposal, an arrangement not unknown in past city administrations.

In early 1979, the mayor and I agreed that it was time for a 10 percent increase in the basic allowance—if the cost would be borne exclusively by the state—and urged such action on the state legislature.* I also favored indexing the basic allowance. But I was never forgiven for withholding support in 1978. Roger Wilkins noted in an article published in the *New York Times* at the end of March 1979: "Dr. Bernstein's critics . . . say that HRA was set up to be the advocate both inside and outside the Administration for service to recipients and that her refusal to press for an increase in the basic welfare grant last year . . . demonstrate[s] the opposite of pro-client advocacy."

Perhaps the single most important requirement for good policy determination and good management in a large organization running complicated programs is highly competent top staff members in each of the major divisions. HRA, or the social welfare agency in any major city, is a *very* large organization. Not only did HRA have a total of almost 25,000 employees, but the smallest of its program divisions had a staff of 600, and the largest had almost 8,000 employees. A major business in New York City is defined as one with 200 or more employees. On any one day, HRA serves a million and a half people in a range of programs—public assistance, food stamps, Medicaid, foster care of children, home-attendant services to the aged and disabled, day care for children, and many others. All must operate within the framework of different laws and regulations and different eligibility criteria. Crises, which may result from a heavy snowstorm, a breakdown in a computer system due to a water failure in the building, or a bullet ricocheting into an HRA office from someone doing target practice on a nearby roof, are a

---

*Stanley Fink, Speaker of the Assembly, made strenuous efforts to achieve legislative approval but without success, against the opposition of Governor Carey and the Republican majority in the state Senate.

part of every week—if not every day. The administrative complexities are immense. Without highly competent top staff, chaos ensues: clients are badly served, staff is demoralized, and vendors, whether they are dentists providing care to Medicaid clients or suppliers of equipment, are not paid and threaten to disrupt or discontinue service.

What I found during my early days at HRA was a mixed picture, indeed: some very good deputies and some who clearly were in positions beyond their capacities; some who regarded their role as that of public servant, and some who thought it appropriate to be an advocate for one social, ethnic, or religious group or another; some who could easily share my approach to welfare administration, and some who felt it was not unreasonable to manipulate the rules if the result was that more money went to the welfare client.

I began to make some changes in personnel after I had been in office a few months and had had the opportunity to appraise the abilities of the top staff members. I did so within the framework of the mayor's directive to all commissioners to find and appoint blacks and Hispanics to top positions, but not to appoint or promote anyone just because he was a member of a minority group or to achieve any quota. In the course of making a series of staff changes, I increased the proportion of blacks in the top positions. But I made the appointments on the basis of my judgment of the individual's competence to do the job, and not on the basis of political relationships or ideology; this was not satisfactory to the black leaders. Their goal was the appointment of black staff members who would be advocates for the black community and—it must be said—would reflect their political patronage; these would be "real" blacks.

I must stress at this point that it is not easy to find highly competent people with a demonstrated work record—whether white, black, or any other color—who are ready to take jobs with the city government at city pay levels. Not only are pay levels in business and industry substantially higher, but so are federal salaries for the kind of top staff one tries to recruit for HRA. Further, one must anticipate a certain amount of public abuse as a local official at the deputy level, something unlikely in federal or state employment—where public abuse is generally reserved for cabinet officers or commissioners—and almost unheard of in business or industry.*

Among the policy decisions I made, none incurred more of a firestorm than an effort to set up a project designed to improve housing accommodations for welfare clients. The demonstration project involved the use of a two-party check for rent, made out to the welfare client and the landlord and cashable by the landlord only when signed by both parties. The two-party check does place a restriction on the client; he cannot either temporarily or permanently use it for other purposes and either delay the payment for rent or not pay it at all. In return for this assurance of rent payments, however, the landlord would guarantee appropriate building maintenance. The effort to do the project was ultimately stifled by a coalition of special interest welfare groups, despite its widespread support from the mayor, other officials, the major newspapers, civic organizations, and groups concerned about low-income housing.[5]

During all of 1978, the mayor publicly and privately proclaimed his steady support for the course I was following. In a year-end roundup with some *New York Post* reporters, he said I had reduced the welfare rolls to the lowest levels in ten years and added, "Now some people don't like that. But that's her

---

*I had instituted some reorganization of the agency to eliminate a situation in which sixteen department heads reported to the commissioner and fourteen subdepartment heads reported to the Deputy for Management. In the process, I created the position of Deputy for Program Operations, to match on the program side the Deputy for Management. It took almost a year to find a qualified person ready to forgo the easier living in Albany, Princeton, or Washington to take on this ten-hour-a-day job at $46,000 a year. Similarly, I had always been critical of the research and analytical capability in HRA and was not less so when I was commissioner; but, again, it took the better part of a year to find the qualified person ready to take the job at $42,000. (Salaries have increased since December 1978.)

job. It's to her credit, but it makes a lot of enemies." The pressure, however, was building. During the first year of the Koch administration, numerous articles, in which my name almost always figured, had been written on the bitter relations between the mayor and the black community, and this climate continued into 1979. Mayor Koch became unhappy with the situation, and it seemed appropriate for me to resign.

I returned to the New School for Social Research and to writing and research. In particular, I began to write a book which would seek to explain certain trends in the development of social welfare programs over the last twenty years—trends which have, unfortunately, served to bring these programs into disrepute. It should not have happened this way; it need not have happened this way.

It is not news that, in a democracy, groups with different values, different notions about the appropriate solutions for problems, or even different views about which problems are more important and more demanding of close attention, contend with each other for political power and influence in shaping policy and in the way programs are administered. It has been the strength of the democratic system that, by and large, the results of the legislative, regulatory, and administrative processes reflected the general consensus and were satisfactory to the electorate. When they are not, a change in leadership at the federal, state, or local level is likely to occur.

Much has been written lately about the decline in the proportion of the electorate which votes and the concomitant rise in the number and influence of special interest groups, some with exceedingly narrow or single interests. The threat to the democratic process is real and grounds for growing concern.

What is fascinating about welfare politics is that, for most of the last two decades, it was dominated by groups with a particular set of values which, it turns out, were not and are not in consonance with generally held values. The policy and administrative results have exacerbated tensions in the society, especially during the last few years of declining economic growth.

Further, in my view, the values which prevailed in the administration of the programs, in contrast to stated legislative policy and intent, fostered dependency instead of reducing it. Efforts to counter trends which appeared to many as undesirable were hampered by proponents of the values which dominated social welfare administration. They appeared to hold the high moral ground, wrapping themselves as they did and do in the mantle of concern for the poor and their belief that only they should be regarded as understanding the needs of the poor. Critics who dwelled on matters such as high rates of ineligibility or the adverse effects of welfare on incentives to work were quickly labeled reactionary, if not racist, and vigorously opposed.

The election of Ronald Reagan in 1980 has brought to the Presidency, the Executive Office, and the Department of Health and Human Services a new outlook and a new approach to problems of social welfare. The change represents a turn of close to 180 degrees in attitudes and values. Legislation proposed by the Reagan administration and largely adopted by the Congress reflects this change. Has it gone—or will it go—too far?

In the chapters which follow, I shall recount developments over the last two decades, through 1981, in the public assistance and related work programs, in child support, and in the food stamp program. The policies and administration of these programs can contribute to continuing dependency or promote efforts to achieve economic and social independence. I shall also discuss important issues which need to be addressed in the future. My focus will be on (1) the interrelationships among legislative policy, executive regulations, and administration or management at the local level, (2) how administration can circumvent legislative policy, and (3) how executive regulation and local administration are influenced at all levels of government, but particularly at the local level, by pressures from special interest groups and the ideology of particular officials. The primary focus will be the experience of New York City, but the politics of welfare in New York are similar in many ways to the politics of welfare in other major urban centers throughout the country.

The general public needs to understand better how welfare programs have developed and how they have gone astray, and what actions can be taken to achieve the humanitarian goals of assisting the poor and vulnerable—goals shared by most Americans. Discussion of the issues and the exercise of influence on the decisions made should not be left to special interest groups of the right or the left. The *via media* is not a very wide road, and yet it is rarely crowded. It is my hope that this book will be a marker toward that middle road. That is what it is designed to do.

CHAPTER 2

What Caused the Welfare Mess?

Welfare, or public assistance, has been the subject of prolonged and heated debate for two decades now, and it is unlikely either that the debate will stop or its heat diminish in the near future. The subject will not go away; widespread recognition of the necessity for financial support for those unable to provide for themselves remains in uneasy coexistence with widespread dissatisfaction with the program and its consequences. Polls taken over recent years found that a large majority (from 70 to 90 percent) supported programs to help the poor and that an almost equally large majority expressed concern or dissatisfaction with welfare programs.

Efforts will continue to be made, as they have since the 1960s, to "reform" welfare—a phrase with quite different meanings for different groups. "Reform" to some will mean a reduction in ineligibility and a work requirement and to others a guaranteed income and the choice of working or not. The motivation for these efforts lies in the view held by both proponents of a liberal welfare system and its detractors that the current system is a mess. As I have indicated, the efforts aimed at major reform of the program have, in my view, been misguided because what caused the mess in the first place has been inadequately understood.

As one reviews congressional debates and legislation—passed or withdrawn—and the record of public discussion about the "welfare mess," three major issues emerge. These are: (1) the level of ineligibility and over- and underpayments; (2) the level of the welfare standard and related benefits such as food stamps and Medicaid; and (3) the impact of the welfare package on incentives to work and ways of dealing with the disincentives when they were recognized to exist.

How one viewed these issues, whether one agreed that ineligibility was in fact a problem, or if it was, whether it was possible to do anything about it short of complete reform of the welfare system; whether the welfare grant was too high, or too low, or reasonable, or even what the actual level of the grant was, as well as the other major issues of work and long-term dependency reflected different basic views. The underlying differences were over the appropriate goals of a welfare program, the degree of individual responsibility which should be demanded of welfare clients, the ability of the economic system to provide jobs suitable to people's skills, and, in response to the protest movement of the sixties, how to improve the lot of minority groups, particularly blacks, who had long suffered from discrimination.

There are many other issues one could discuss, especially the sharing of the financial burden of welfare among federal, state, and local levels of government, the appropriate level of government to administer the system, and the sometimes unnecessary complexity of the current system. But I shall limit myself to the three issues noted above, because they are most closely related to the emergence of the notion of a "welfare mess" and to the basic question of long-term dependency. For it is my view that not only legislative policies but, in significant measure, the way the system was administered in many urban areas of the country, particularly in New York City, for too many years, led to an increase in long-term dependency. I also believe that the "welfare mess" can be greatly minimized, if not largely eliminated, by appropriate legislative policy and, above all, by good administration; "welfare reform" as it was proposed in the Nixon and Carter administrations or, in more colorful words, welfare reform with bands playing and flags flying, should not be necessary. It is useful to start with some figures on the nature and growth of the welfare caseload during the past two decades.

By far the largest of the welfare programs is Aid to Families with Dependent Children (AFDC), which is financed by the federal, state, and sometimes also local governments. It serves almost exclusively female-headed families, except for a small proportion of families with disabled fathers. In the country as a whole, the number of recipients rose from just under 3 million in 1960 to a peak of 10.8 million in 1976. Until 1967, the annual rate of increase ranged between 4.4 and 7.9 percent. Double-digit annual increases began in 1968 and lasted through 1972, ranging from 13.2 percent to a high of 26.2 percent in 1971.[1] The AFDC caseload in New York State, however, driven mainly by New York City, began to show double-digit increases four years earlier, in 1963. In that year it rose 12.9 percent, and increased to a peak of 24.4 percent in 1968, the year New York City's caseload rose 26.3 percent. Among states comparable to New York in terms of size of population and degree of urbanization, California and Massachusetts exhibited a pattern similar to New York's. In the sixties their caseloads also rose sharply, though not quite as much as in New York, but their double-digit increases continued in 1972. Michigan and Pennsylvania are closer to the national pattern; double-digit increases began in 1966 and lasted through 1973.

In the period from 1974 through 1980, caseloads mainly declined slightly; they sometimes rose, but again only slightly. Generally, the changes were between 1.5 and 4.3 percent. In all five states and New York City, AFDC caseloads in 1980 were below the peak levels reached between 1972 and 1977. Michigan, however, is close to its peak, reflecting the especially heavy unemployment in the automobile industry. Nevertheless, the caseloads remain high, as the following tabulation of the number of AFDC recipients indicates:[2]

AFDC Recipients (in thousands)
(Excluding AFDC-U)

	PEAK YEAR	1980
United States (1976)	10,795	9,986
New York State (1972)	1,251	1,058
New York City (1972)	888	734
California (1972)	1,295	1,201
Massachusetts (1977)	347	329
Michigan (1976)	595	590
Pennsylvania (1972)	634	590

The AFDC-U program covers families in which the father is present in the home but is unemployed or employed less than 100 hours per month.* Less than half of the states have established this program; in those states which have AFDC-U, it has generally been less than 10 percent of the total AFDC caseload, except in Michigan and California. In New York State, at its peak in 1968, it equaled 10 percent of the caseload; in 1979, it was 4 percent.

Mention should also be made of the General Assistance program, financed exclusively by state and local funds, for intact families and single individuals. Again, less than half of all states have such programs, and some of those which do have narrowed eligibility for single individuals in recent years. Data available for New York State and New York City indicate divergent trends for families and single individuals. In both state and city, the number of recipients in family units grew by 50 percent between 1960 and 1971, when it peaked. Since then this number has rapidly dropped. In contrast, the single caseload leapt upward in the years 1963 to 1968, increasing fivefold in the city, though it grew only by 50 percent in the rest of the state. After a five-year pause, even some decline, it again jumped

---

*As a result of a recent court decision, if the wife is the primary earner in the family, the family could be eligible for AFDC-U if she is unemployed or employed less than 100 hours per month.

in 1974 to 1977, years of recession in the city, reaching a new peak. Since then, the caseload has stabilized at only slightly below its highest level in the city and at about 18 percent below its peak in the rest of the state. In 1980, about 91,000 single persons were on welfare in the city, and about 30,000 in the rest of the state.

What is noteworthy about these trends is that the big jumps in caseload occurred mainly during periods of increasing prosperity and declining unemployment. These data provide the framework within which to consider the three major issues in the congressional and public debate over welfare.

INELIGIBILITY AND OVERPAYMENTS

A review of the *New York Times* over the last twenty years reveals widespread concern about the number of ineligible people on welfare.* Indeed, if there has been any single factor responsible for the general public perception of welfare as a mess, it has been the sense that ineligibility was too high. As early as July 1960, James Dumpson, Commissioner of Welfare in 1959–1965, responded to criticism on this score by noting that his agency had the authority "to weed out freeloaders and we do it." In January 1962, he voiced his "wholehearted" support of a proposal to have the state help the city cope with relief frauds, but insisted that the city already had "a tight procedure to detect relief fraud." This was the period during which the caseload was low, about a quarter of a million persons or about 3 percent of the city's population; home visits, which later were stopped, were still being made, and significant efforts were undertaken to check on ineligibility. The situation was soon to change. (So was Dumpson's attitude toward the ineligibility problem when he returned to the commissioner's post in 1974–1975; see the discussion later in this chapter.)

---

*Unless otherwise noted, all quotations in this section were reported in the *New York Times*.

During the mid-sixties, the welfare caseload in New York began to grow at an accelerating rate. But despite the apparent inconsistency between sharply rising caseloads and the improving economic situation, welfare officials maintained that ineligibility was not a problem, insisting that it did not exceed the officially tolerable limit of 3 percent. Indeed, in his first year in office Mitchell Ginsberg, HRA commissioner in 1966 to 1970, lectured caseworkers over closed-circuit television to the effect that there were more persons in the city eligible for welfare and not receiving it than there were on the rolls.[3] In 1966 to 1967, a move was led by Ginsberg and others in the social welfare community in New York and throughout the country to eliminate home visits and investigations as demeaning to welfare clients and, in their view, unnecessary to ensure the integrity of the system. They proposed instead to rely on a self-declaration of need by the welfare applicant and on spot checks to determine the validity of the applications.

Other factors were at play. This was the period of the height of the influence of Richard Cloward, the intellectual leader of a radical movement for welfare rights, and of the National Welfare Rights Organization, under the direction of the late Dr. George Wiley. It was also the period of concern about the riots in the streets of Watts, Washington, and other cities, and of efforts to ameliorate the economic and social position of blacks and other minority groups. On the New York City scene, the unrest manifested itself in rancorous and riotous behavior in the welfare centers, encouraged and orchestrated by various welfare rights groups. Clients demanded quick approval of their applications or special grants for clothing, household furnishings, or other items. The welfare rights groups were aided and abetted by the city's caseworkers' union. One former HRA official observed that "it became something of a badge of honor for caseworkers to manipulate the regulations to build the largest possible grant for a client."[4]

Federal welfare officials were sympathetic to the call for more dignified treatment of welfare recipients. In 1968 a federal regulation was issued which promulgated the use of the self-declaration and, in effect, eliminated home visits to verify eligibility. In a sense, this regulation contradicted congressional intent. Already disturbed by the rise in the caseload nationally between 1960 and 1967, Congress enacted legislation in 1967 that set a ceiling on the number of AFDC recipients in each state at the level which would be reached in 1968 (later amended to 1969). Throughout the country, but particularly in the Northeast and the West, many state welfare administrators, concerned about the potential impact of the cap at some time in the future, wanted as high a ceiling as possible. A less rigorous review of applications for welfare was instituted, made official by the regulation on the self-declaration. The introduction of the self-declaration was followed by further large increases in the welfare caseload in New York and many other states, and by substantial increases in the ineligibility rates.

The new system was hailed by both Wyman, state Commissioner of Social Services, and HRA commissioner Ginsberg, who noted his particular satisfaction with "the fact that it had been tested with satisfactory results here in the city." In fact, the test results, though from a study by an outside consultant, proved to be wrong, but this was not to become crystal-clear for some years.

There followed a period of some five years, from 1968 through 1972, during which Ginsberg and his successor as of 1970, Jules Sugarman, insisted, despite evidence to the contrary, that ineligibility did not exceed the tolerable limit of 3 percent. For example, a study by the Department of Health, Education, and Welfare (HEW), based on a sample of cases obtaining welfare in the period from November 1968 through January 1969, indicated that as many as 30 percent of cases were ineligible or obtaining overpayments. Ginsberg disputed these findings. In March 1972, the state's Welfare Inspector General, George Berlinger, issued a report estimating a rate of 10 to 15 percent ineligibility. Sugarman denounced Berlinger for "reckless irresponsibility" and "inexcusable politicizing" and contended that the real ineligibility rate was 3 percent or less.*

*One trouble, among others, with the city quality control audits was that the ineligibility figure was based on only half the original sample. The

In the first article I wrote on the welfare problem in New York City, early in 1970, I questioned both the ineligibility estimates issued by city officials and the estimates of persons who had not applied for welfare, though they were presumptively eligible. I also charged that a permissive atmosphere engendered by the self-declaration and the rhetoric of welfare officials was encouraging excessive dependence on welfare. I pointed out that the government does not rely on a taxpayer's self-declaration for income tax purposes, but checks income through the W-2 form and other means. I added, "There is no reason to believe that the poor are less honest than the relatively well-to-do, but there is no reason to believe that they are more honest either.[5] In another study done a year later, I found no vast reservoir of eligible families who had not applied for welfare and, indeed, found evidence that as many as 60,000 persons receiving welfare were ineligible.[6] Both welfare officials and the Community Council of Greater New York, representing many of the social welfare organizations in the city, were critical of the report; and both reiterated the official 3 percent figure.

Governor Nelson Rockefeller and other state officials, however, were becoming increasingly uneasy about the size of the caseload and the accumulating evidence of high rates of ineligibility and overpayments. In July 1971, a new Rockefeller-sponsored law came into effect, requiring employable recipients to pick up their welfare checks at offices of the New York State Employment Services (NYSES). It also required clients to register with NYSES and accept job referrals and job offers, if any, in order to maintain continued eligibility for welfare grants. The results were fairly shocking: about 20 percent of the clients did not pick up their checks during the first cycle. Hopes that this was a temporary phenomenon due to misunderstanding or administrative snafus were dashed as the figure remained at this level through several succeeding cycles. It eventually declined to a stable rate of 7 to 8 percent. Many cases were closed as a

other half of cases in the sample were "indeterminate"—that is, sufficient information had not been developed to determine whether they were eligible or not. That, of course, was where the problem lay buried.

result.* Despite the evidence, the Community Council, reflecting the views of the social welfare community, called in September 1972 for repeal of the law, contending that a "high percentage of unemployable recipients were being forced to divert money needed for food and clothing to carfare to NYSES and job interviews."

While Commissioner Sugarman continued well into 1972 to maintain that ineligibility was no more than 3 to 4 percent, neither he nor Mayor John Lindsay was altogether happy with the situation. Though Lindsay did not express concern over the ineligibility issue publicly, he apparently did so within his official family. He made funds available for hiring top management staff to develop additional procedures for reducing fraud and abuse and for a substantially expanded computer operation. But for whatever reasons, the efforts of management staff to expand and improve the computer operation never got off the ground, and other efforts to reduce ineligibility and overpayments had only minimal effects. And then plain old-fashioned politics intervened.

Among the most significant steps which Sugarman took to improve the integrity of the program was a demonstration project instituted in three welfare centers. Mail recertification (by which the client sent in a card stating his continued eligibility for welfare) was replaced by "face-to-face recertification" (FFR). The client was required to report to the center for an interview and a review of his eligibility status. The results were startling: the level of ineligibility ranged from about 13 to 18 percent in the three centers.

Even more startling to some of us who had been concerned for some time about the potentially high ineligibility rate was that, instead of immediately expanding the program to all the other welfare centers, Sugarman decided first to computerize and centralize the program in special FFR centers. The demonstration program was stopped, but the new program did not get

---

*The impact on the total caseload would have been more dramatic except that, because of a court ruling, it could be applied only to General Assistance cases and not generally to those on AFDC.

under way for a year; even then it was only on a minor scale.[7] One can argue the merits of centralized versus decentralized FFR systems, although later evidence indicated a decentralized system was more effective. But one can state with some certitude that the spring of 1972 was not a politically convenient time to purge the welfare rolls of the high proportion of ineligibles, who were mainly members of the black and Puerto Rican minorities in the city. Mayor Lindsay was making his run in the Democratic presidential primaries, and among his important constituencies were these same groups.

In the meantime, the New York State Department of Social Services (NYSDSS) had already initiated a change in the application procedure in 1972, replacing the short-form self-declaration by an eleven-page form that required considerable documentation before a final determination of eligibility was made. The department also took over the responsibility for the semiannual quality control audits from the city. A more thorough and complete job was done. Official results were that in the second half of 1973, ineligibility in New York City as well as upstate was over 18 percent; overpayments were at 35 percent; and underpayments, at about 9 percent. The state had already mandated face-to-face recertifications in place of mail recertification, and in April 1973 it had warned local welfare departments that they faced fiscal penalties if they failed to comply with the mandate. A significant reduction in ineligibility, however, was not to be achieved for some time to come, although a small decrease in caseload occurred in 1973–1974 as a result of the use of a photo ID for check cashing identification, a reduction in the number of duplicate checks issued, and a few other efforts to improve the administration of the program.

With the return of James Dumpson as HRA commissioner under Mayor Abraham Beame's administration in January 1974, the official rhetoric in the city continued to de-emphasize ineligibility problems and re-emphasized those who were eligible but had not applied. In a statement in March 1974, Dumpson said, "One out of every three New Yorkers can be considered needy [with incomes below the Bureau of Labor Statistics lower-level living standard] and although one in six New Yorkers is currently on welfare perhaps as many as another half million could also be on the rolls." This estimate was highly questionable, to say the least. In any event, while the state audits showed some decline in ineligibility and overpayments in 1974 from a payment-error rate of 27.4 percent to 25.0 percent, it was still far too high, and the caseload began rising again in late 1974.

It was the fiscal crisis in New York City which provided the political framework and the impetus for a determined effort to reduce fraud and abuse. A necessary ingredient was the appointment of officials to direct NYSDSS—Stephen Berger, and later Philip Toia, as commissioner, and myself as Deputy Commissioner for Income Maintenance—who believed that the job could be done, that it was necessary to do it, and who were prepared to give the effort high priority and continued attention. There is no magic wand which will reduce fraud and abuse. It takes a series of management initiatives and constant attention to administrative detail, and it takes computers to accomplish many of the tasks which would otherwise be too time-consuming and expensive as hand operations.

Among the first activities undertaken was a "mail-out." A one-page questionnaire was sent to all welfare cases (AFDC and General Assistance recipients) asking if they still needed welfare and, if so, to provide updated information on family composition, earnings if any, and other data. The results were of considerable interest. First, about 1,000 cases advised that they no longer needed welfare. But the main and substantial savings came from those who did not respond to the questionnaire or to the subsequent notice of closing of the case. The cost of this effort was minimal and the savings large. During 1975–1977, each mail-out resulted in more than 10,000 case closings, of which about half remained closed for six months or more. It was soon made a regular semiannual procedure, and in 1978 was placed on a four-month cycle.* The September 1980 mail-out resulted

---

*HRA undertook such a mail-out in early 1974 and obtained good results but did not make it standard procedure or even repeat it. Some regarded it as "hassling" the clients.

in notification from over 1,800 cases that they no longer needed assistance, and 6,750 cases were closed because they did not respond to the notice of closing or because their whereabouts were unknown. Estimated annual savings run to many millions of dollars, and the costs are less than $250,000 per mail-out.

The face-to-face recertification procedure in HRA was in a parlous state in 1975. About 25 percent of the cases were not on the computer and so had not been called in for an interview at all; of those who were called in, many were not interviewed because of inadequate staffing and mis-scheduling of interviews. Improvement did not come quickly or without recriminations, as well as cooperation, between state and city staff, but it did come.* Again, the savings result mainly from the cases which can be closed because of failure to respond to the notice of interview or to the closing notice. In 1977, 97,000 cases were closed, and again about half remained closed for at least six months; these constituted about 44 percent of all closings. In 1980, the figure was 61,000, or 31.5 percent of all closings.

The results of the mail-out and the FFR interviews reveal an interesting aspect of the attitude of welfare clients toward the grant. It is rare, indeed, for welfare clients to write or call in to say that they have found a job, or married or remarried, or that the husband has returned to the home and that they are glad to tell us they do not need welfare any more or, alternatively, do not need as large a grant. But faced with an official interview or paper which must be signed, many thousands of clients will simply not respond or turn up. This is how they tell the welfare department that they do not need welfare anymore. They do not offer the information any sooner than the system makes it necessary for them to do so. After all, even if one finds a job, it is nice to have several hundred extra dollars a month.

---

*Even at the beginning of 1978, however, staff assigned were insufficient to maintain the semiannual schedule. As HRA commissioner at this point, I was able to persuade the mayor to allow for an increase in FFR staff even within reduced personnel ceilings to restore the semiannual interview and subsequently to achieve a schedule of one interview every four months.

One cannot, however, rely solely on the types of measures just described to reduce ineligibility. In another series of actions, we greatly extended and increased the frequency of the computer matching program. That is, we expanded the matching of the welfare payment file with the files of such payments as social security benefits, unemployment insurance, Supplemental Security Income (SSI), and Veterans Benefits and with a variety of other relevant material, including state and local and Comprehensive Employment and Training Act (CETA) payrolls, marriage licenses issued, lists of children in foster care, and records of persons in prison. Each of these matches reveals some "hits," and on investigation of the recipients a significant proportion is determined to be ineligible. Thus the case can be closed or the grant can be reduced.

As the matching program was expanded, a major missing link became evident—there was no general wage reporting file in New York State. Most states have such a file in connection with their unemployment insurance system, but New York, along with about a dozen other states, operated on a different basis.* In 1978, Governor Carey proposed the establishment of a wage reporting system in New York, under the auspices of the Tax Department, which would match not only the welfare payment file but also the file of unemployment insurance beneficiaries, and others, as appropriate.

Some business leaders opposed the proposal at first, because of the additional cost of preparing the quarterly reports, but most were quickly persuaded when informed of the potential savings on welfare and unemployment insurance. The social welfare community and the civil libertarians, however, maintained a vigorous opposition to the establishment of the system

---

*New York uses a wage requesting system. That is, the wage record is obtained from the last and previous employers only when a person applies for unemployment insurance. Wage reports to the Social Security system are no longer useful, since they were shifted to an annual reporting basis as of January 1979. Annual data are too "stale" for use in matching.

on the grounds of invasion of privacy—despite the obvious provisions in the legislation to safeguard the confidentiality of the information. They were, of course, less concerned about potential savings in welfare or unemployment insurance payments. The legislation was adopted, and each quarterly match since the system went into operation has resulted in substantial savings through case closings or reductions in grants: about 1,000 permanent case closings and 1,700 cases which are rebudgeted for estimated annual cost saving of more than $5 million.

The net result of all these efforts—mail-outs, FFR interviews, and computer matching—is that ineligibility has been reduced from the peak of 18 percent in 1973 and the still-high level of over 13 percent in 1975 to about 5 percent in the period between October 1979 and March 1980. Similarly, overpayments have gone down from a high of 35 percent to 15 percent. The overall payment-error rate was brought down from 25 percent in 1974 to as low as 7.7 percent in October 1979–March 1980. In the subsequent six-month period, April through September 1980, however, the ineligibility rate rose to 6.7 percent, overpayments rose to 16.4, and the payment-error rate rose to 9.7 percent. In dollar terms, even at this higher rate, the waste in the program was reduced from an annual rate of $218 million to $72 million, allowing for a tolerable error rate of 4 percent. The record on underpayments has not improved, but it remains fairly low. The total caseload declined from just over one million persons in 1974–1975 to about 875,000 in 1980, even though unemployment rose from 7 percent in 1974 to almost 11 percent in 1976 and remained at 8 to 10 percent in 1980. (Total welfare payments rose from $1.039 billion in 1974 to $1.264 billion in 1980, despite the decline in the total caseload—mainly because of the increase in payments for rent, which constitute, on average, more than a third of the total welfare grant.)

In sum, New York City, which for almost two decades was widely regarded as the symbol of the welfare mess, now has a moderately good record. The rise in the payment-error rate to 9.7 percent during April through September 1980 and the subsequent six-month period however, and a further rise to 10.3 percent* in April–September 1981, are disturbing. These developments underline the necessity for continued vigilance, constant attention to administrative detail, and further improvements in techniques for detecting abuse. Indeed, there is no reason to believe that the poor are less adept at manipulating welfare than the rich are at manipulating the income tax system.

THE LEVEL OF THE WELFARE STANDARD

The controversy which swirls over the level of the welfare standard—is it too high? too low? is it adequate or inadequate?—is, in part, a definitional problem which arises out of the plethora of existing programs designed to aid the poor. In part, however, it reflects a deliberate effort by partisan groups to belittle the size of the welfare package.

In a sense, there is no single welfare program, though welfare is frequently regarded as synonymous with the public assistance programs, AFDC, AFDC-U, and General Assistance. Provision for the welfare of those with no income or insufficient income is made through a mixture of programs—some in cash, some in kind—to cover the needs for food, shelter, clothing, and other items such as electricity and fuel, transportation, home furnishings, and medical care. It is done through public assistance, food stamps, school lunches, special energy allowances, and Medicaid.

Since 1971, a basic allowance, determined in New York by the state legislature, covers food, clothing, and other miscellaneous items other than shelter or medical care. This allowance is standardized in relation to family size throughout the state. The amounts received by a family of four from all sources are as follows:

Basic allowance. Until July 1, 1981, the basic allowance, last increased in 1974 on the basis of 1972 prices, was $258

*Preliminary figure.

per month. This figure has now been raised to $297 per month.*

Rent. In addition, a separate cash grant covers rent as paid up to a maximum of $218 for a family of four in New York City—a figure established by NYSDSS in 1975.

Food stamps. In addition, a family of four (which in 1972 received $30 in food stamps—the "bonus" value, or value beyond what they paid for the stamps) received $125 per month in food stamps at the beginning of 1981, assuming they had no income other than the public assistance grant.

School lunches. In addition, if there are school-age children in the family, they receive free school lunches, which cost about $1.08 per lunch, or $17 per month averaged for the whole year.** Or, if they are below school age, children may benefit from other free food programs in day-care centers or other facilities or from the Women, Infants, and Children (WIC) program.

*An increase of 15 percent was voted by the state legislature and approved by Governor Carey, effective July 1, 1981, raising the basic allowance to $297 per month. The relationship between income (or welfare grant) and the food stamp allotment, however, created an anomalous situation. An increase in the cash grant will ordinarily result in a reduction in food stamps, so that the net benefit to the client may be only about half of what it otherwise would be. State authorities have labeled the increase as a payment to cover increased fuel costs in an effort to exclude it from the definition of income for food stamp calculations, but it is highly doubtful that federal approval will be obtained. Negotiations were still under way as of January 1982 between NYSDSS and the federal authorities. While the issue is still in doubt, the state's cause has been aided by legislation approved by Congress late in 1981 which generally exempts cash grants specifically designed for utility payments if they run for no more than six months. The Secretary of Agriculture may, however, waive the six months limitation if it is not administratively feasible; the state has claimed that it is not.

**The Reagan proposals for budget cuts provided for the adjustment of the food stamp allotment if school-age children are eligible for free school lunches, but this provision was dropped in the congressional negotiations on the bill and was not included in the final legislation.

Fuel costs. In addition, in New York City, families with children receive $150 as a one-time payment to cover in-
creased fuel costs, even though almost all are renters and
do not pay fuel costs directly. (Upstate, the allowance is
$250, and many clients live in houses and pay for their
own fuel.)

Medical care. Finally, in addition, the welfare family receives free medical services, which required in 1980 an
average expenditure from Medicaid funds of approximately $1,200 per AFDC family of four. This sum is only
$120 below the amount expended for medical care out of
income by the average family of four with an income
equal to the Bureau of Labor Statistics (BLS) lower-level
living standard ($14,393 in the New York area in autumn
1980 prices, including $11,374 for consumption expendi-
tures; the remaining $3,019 goes for income and social
security taxes, gifts and contributions, etc.).

These various grants in cash or in kind to a four-person
family on welfare add up to $730 per month, assuming one child
obtains free school lunches, or $8,760 per year, a sum equal to
88 percent of the BLS lower-level budget for consumption expenditures.* It should also be noted that a substantial part of
the welfare package is indexed, either specifically or in effect.
Food stamps are indexed to the cost of food, and allotments have
been raised semiannually and will continue to be raised on an
annual basis; rents are, in effect, indexed up to the maximum
for each family size;** school lunches and, more important,
medical care are, in effect, indexed, since the welfare family
pays nothing for the service even though the cost rises inexora-
bly each year.

---

*As a result of the 15 percent increase in the basic allowance, this figure
rose by approximately $300 to $470 as of July 1, 1981, depending on the final
decision regarding the definition of income for calculating the food stamp allotment. The BLS lower-level budget has been adjusted for a family of one
adult and three children instead of two adults and two children.

**Even in 1980, only 21 percent of the welfare caseload was above the
maximum, and among these are some families who are benefiting from the

Thus the welfare family's economic picture, though not one of luxury, is similar to that of an independent working family of modest means. But one would never know it from the public statements of leaders of the social welfare community or welfare advocacy groups beginning around 1974 and continuing with increasing stridency through 1981. Commissioner Dumpson was especially partial to asking audiences the rhetorical question, "How can anyone expect a family of four to live on $258 a month?" The response that no one did expect a family of four to do that did not change his rhetoric, which he believed would be more effective in promoting an increase in the basic allowance than would a full account of the package.

At the end of 1974, the Community Council urged the legislature to increase the basic allowance for a family of four from $258 to $384 a month, exclusive of rent and fuel, ignoring as it did so all other benefits accruing to the welfare family. Only in the last few years has the Community Council taken account of the increasing food stamp bonus in its analysis of the deterioration of the basic allowance due to inflation and become somewhat more moderate in its demands.

Refusal to take any account of the value of medical care continues, as evidenced by an eruption of responses to a letter I wrote to the *New York Times* in late November 1980. I pointed out the need to look at all the elements of the welfare package and not just the basic allowance before deciding that welfare grants had been enormously eroded. The writer of an editorial entitled "A Poor Argument about Poor People" charged, "She includes increased Medicaid payments when determining the impact of inflation," as if I were saying the sicker, the better. Dumpson, in his letter published in early December, made the odd argument that I "misrepresented the shelter allowance as income" and that "Medicaid is not income but an expenditure

$30 and one-third income disregard and who, therefore, have more income, or who are sharing quarters with non–public assistance family members or friends and in fact are not spending more for rent than they are allowed. The other portion, more than three-quarters of the caseload, could obtain an increased allowance if their rent were raised.

substitute." It is indeed a substitute for the portion of the work-ing family's income spent for medical care, but it cannot be ignored.

It may be argued that in-kind benefits, such as food stamps, school lunches, medical care, or a fixed cash grant for rent, are not as useful as unallocated cash because they are not fungible; they cannot be exchanged for other types of purchases at the choice of the welfare client. This is partly, though not alto-gether, true. For example, welfare clients obtaining food stamps or free school lunches for their children can spend less of the basic cash allowance for food and purchase other items instead; studies have indicated that they do just that. Welfare clients might spend less for rent if the rent grant were combined with the basic allowance; they might double up or choose poorer quarters, but certainly a substantial portion of the rent grant would have to be used to purchase shelter. Medical care, how-ever, is less a matter of choice, unless one is prepared to accept the neglect of health problems, especially for children, if the welfare client would prefer to spend the money that medical services cost in some other way. On the face of it, this does not appear to be good social policy.

Liberals and moderates, and probably many conservatives as well, would agree that those in need should be provided with assistance sufficient for an adequate level of living. The dis-agreement arises on the issue of defining "adequate." The six-ties were characterized by an expanding economy and a general assumption that it would continue to expand indefinitely, by the pressure and heat generated by the riots in many urban areas, by constant demonstrations by the National Welfare Rights Organization, by a heightened sense of guilt over continuing discrimination against blacks and other minorities, and by pres-sure from several court decisions. In this liberal atmosphere, the New York legislature decided to define "adequate" as the equivalent of the BLS lower-level living standard when it estab-lished a single statewide standard in 1971 to replace a myriad of special grants. (The legislature had increased grant levels regu-larly during the 1960s. Between 1964 and 1968, annual grants increased at an average rate of 8 percent per year, faster than cost-of-living or wage increases.)

The standard was adjusted for the usual composition of a welfare family (one adult and one or more children); some downward adjustments were made in relatively minor categories of expenditures; and, as indicated, medical care was covered separately through Medicaid. The level of consciousness about food stamps was low, although this program was just on the verge of a tremendous expansion and higher benefits. The availability and value of food stamps, as well as school lunches, was ignored in setting the cash allowance.

It is doubtful that most legislators were really aware of how high a standard they were setting. In 1972 prices, the package for public assistance, food stamps, school lunches, and Medicaid for the four-person family was equivalent to a gross income of $7,000 per year. It matched the gross earnings of a worker earning about $3.80 per hour for a thirty-five-hour week, more than a substantial number of workers were making at that time. In 1980 prices, it is the equivalent of a gross income of more than $11,000, requiring an hourly wage of close to $6.00 per hour—again more than a substantial number of workers earn. It is a standard which is achieved, on average, only if there are 1.3 wage earners in the four-person family.

It was this kind of analysis and calculation of the value of the whole welfare package which upset many liberals and the social welfare community when it was first published in 1972, since it left in tatters, if it did not completely destroy, the picture of a welfare family desperately and unsuccessfully trying to make ends meet on $258 per month. Moreover, it greatly diminished the potential for success of the campaign begun in 1974 to persuade the legislature to increase the basic allowance. Not until the legislative session of 1981 did the prospect for an increase of 10 to 15 percent become realistic. The Consumer Price Index had increased about 70 percent since 1972, and it was time for some adjustment in the basic allowance in the full knowledge of the value of food stamps and other benefits available to the welfare family.

Why did the welfare advocates and the leaders of the social welfare community keep urging an increase from the mid-1970s on, in the face of the available information about the value of the welfare package? One answer is that they were convinced of the rightness of their cause; they believe—it is a matter of faith—that the welfare family should receive the BLS lower-level standard and are unconcerned that, on average, it takes 1.3 wage earners per four-person family to achieve this standard. Another answer is that they are a special interest group whose appeal lies with a special constituency. If they are not advocates, they lose identity, power, and influence as they merge with a wider group.

In New York, as in many other industrialized, urban states, the welfare package provides a standard of living which can be achieved for the family of four only by a wage substantially above the minimum of $3.35 per hour. We now need to examine the whole issue of the relationship of welfare and work, the impact of the welfare package on incentives to work, and how the debate has been conducted on the incentive issue and the question of whether welfare mothers should work.

WORK AND WELFARE: THE ISSUE OF INCENTIVES TO WORK

When the Social Security Act was passed in 1935, establishing the Aid to Families with Dependent Children (AFDC) Program, it was assumed that the widows or the wives of disabled workers whom it was designed to help were needed at home and would not ordinarily work. This made good sense at the time; the technology of cooking, cleaning, and washing was such that homemaking was a full-time job. Fewer than 10 percent of married women were in the labor force, and it was generally assumed that married women would not work after marriage, especially after the first child was born. Starting with World War II, however, the role of married women in the labor force changed dramatically, for both women with children and those without children. Once the trend started, it continued through the next two decades, though it abated in the 1950s. Currently, about 60 percent of married women in intact families with children six years of age or over are working, as are about 35 percent of mothers with children below school age. Among female-headed families, the comparable figures are approximately 64 and 52 percent.[8]

During the 1950s, the Congress, other public officials, and the public at large were not too concerned about any relationship between welfare and work. Welfare benefits, in real terms, were on the whole low. Neither the food stamp program nor the Medicaid program had been established. Even though welfare caseloads rose from the very low point they reached at the end of World War II, they were not yet so large as to attract attention as a major issue. Only some mild legislation was adopted by Congress to encourage the states to undertake community projects to provide work for AFDC mothers; little came of it.

During the 1960s, beginning in New York and spreading quickly throughout the country, welfare caseloads exploded, the level of welfare grants rose, and official and public concern mounted. It would be inaccurate to say that welfare administrators in New York State or New York City did nothing to promote employment for welfare clients. State officials were promoting some work and training programs. From 1960 through 1977, under the Wagner, Lindsay, and Beame administrations and under the respective welfare commissioners Dumpson, Ginsberg, Sugarman, Dumpson (again), and J. Henry Smith,* the record shows a series of efforts, generally of modest size, to develop work or job training programs. What was curious, however, about most of the efforts in the city and what, in the end, made them ineffective was the accompanying litany—made up of a number of distinct themes—all making it sound as though the effort was not worthwhile, or was too costly, or just was too herculean a task to be managed.

---

*I have omitted Mitchell Sviridoff, the first commissioner of the Human Resources Administration, who was in office only briefly.

The first theme was that very few employable persons were, in fact, on welfare. Dumpson announced in the spring of 1963 that only 1.8 percent of all welfare recipients were employable, a figure rounded to 2 percent at the beginning of 1964. Ginsberg reported in the fall of 1966 that only 8,500 of 560,000 recipients were employable, less than 2 percent. A few months thereafter he expressed his irritation with critics of the welfare program, stating that "no matter how many times I say the great bulk of people on welfare aren't employable, it doesn't make any difference."* Part of the problem was a lack of adequate data on employability, a lack which may, of course, have been due to the absence of any serious effort to obtain the information. But in part it was due to what can only be described as a deliberate effort to minimize the degree of employability of welfare recipients by basing the percentage on the total caseload, including children, even though no serious person in the 1960s expected or wanted children to be put to work. There was, however, a general expectation that heads of household would work and support their children if they were capable of working and if jobs were available.

It was not until Sugarman's tenure that studies completed in 1973 by the Rand Corporation, working cooperatively with HRA, revealed that 35 to 40 percent of the heads of AFDC households were employable—that is, were free of any serious health problems and had children no younger than school age. Further, about half of the women in this category, or about 20 percent of all AFDC cases, had only one or two school-age children; the problem of child care for them would have been minimal.

The second theme sounded the clarion against "menial" jobs. It must be borne in mind that from the mid-1960s until 1970, we were in a period of labor scarcity in the city as well as in most of the country. Despite the loss of thousands of manufacturing jobs, it was difficult to walk down any major street in Manhattan in 1969, or to enter a subway car, without seeing

---

*As in the section on Ineligibility and Overpayments, all quotations in this section, unless otherwise specified, are from the *New York Times.*

help-wanted signs; many of the ads were for unskilled or semi-skilled jobs. Unemployment was down to 3 percent. Yet one cannot find any recognition of this fact by welfare administrators either at the state or at the city level. Rather, one sees complaints about the mismatch of jobs and available skills among welfare recipients and, at the same time, a resistance to requiring recipients to take unskilled jobs. The emphasis is on education and training. As Ginsberg said in early 1967, "We've got to provide job training that will not only qualify these mothers to get jobs but to advance in them."

Part of the problem lies in the confusion caused by the use of the ubiquitous family of four in all discussions of welfare grants and their relationship to wages. The fact is that for some years about half of all AFDC families have been two- or three-person families. A standard of living somewhat better than welfare provided could be achieved with a job paying $4 or $5 per hour. As for single persons on the General Assistance, jobs even at the minimum wage would have provided a higher income than welfare. These facts were somehow lost in all the welfare rhetoric because part of the problem lay in the black-white liberal politics of the period. It somehow became reactionary to insist that employable persons on welfare, mainly blacks and Hispanics, should take unskilled jobs. It was regarded as the stereotype of discrimination against minorities.

Education and training are, indeed, an essential part of any program to reduce dependency, especially for younger mothers and adolescents on welfare. But the question remains whether the welfare client should have the right to reject a job offer even at the minimum wage and retain the choice of remaining on a full welfare grant instead of working. An alternative would have been to require acceptance of low-paying jobs supplemented with partial welfare grants if the wages were insufficient for the family to achieve at least the welfare standard. But somehow this alternative was never seriously considered by welfare officials, although existing law and regulations permitted precisely this type of supplementation. Indeed, one also began to hear that no AFDC mother should be required to take an unskilled or semiskilled job because, as some among the city's welfare

officials figured out, the rate of pay based on the difference between the welfare grant without work and a partial welfare grant
with work came to only 75 cents an hour, and why should one
work for 75 cents an hour? When I first heard this argument,
about 1972, I made some calculations of the comparable earnings of a policeman or a fireman in New York City, married
with three children. It turned out that the policeman or fireman,
under the illusion that he was being paid about $15,000 per year
plus fringe benefits, was really working for $1.75 an hour—the
difference between what he would have obtained on welfare and
what his wages, plus fringe benefits and minus taxes and the
welfare grant, left him and his family. The welfare officials were
not, however, either impressed or moved by this analysis.

The third theme began to be heard in 1966, when it was
becoming increasingly implausible to attribute the continued
rapid increase in caseload to the unavailability of jobs. This
theme stated that it was necessary to provide a financial incentive to encourage AFDC mothers to take jobs. It represented a
major shift in attitudes about the responsibilities of welfare
clients and was to have a major impact on plans for welfare
reform. Heretofore, or at least since it became common for married women with children to work, the underlying policy assumption, if not the practice, was that an AFDC mother should
work if she could and if a job was available. Now the notion of
incentives was taking hold.

Congress began to consider ways to encourage selected
groups of AFDC mothers to work, and in 1967 passed legislation
establishing the Work Incentive (WIN) program. This legislation
had two important features: (1) no AFDC mother was required
to participate in the program, and (2) mothers were offered a
financial incentive to work—the famous $30 and a third disre-
gard. In other words, the first $30 and one-third of the rest of
gross earnings are not taken into account in determining welfare benefits. Further, full deductions are allowed for income
and social security taxes and all work expenses including day
care. This legislation reflected the view that, first, there was no
obligation on the mother's part to work if she did not want to,
and, second, even if she did want to work there was no obli-

gation for her to do so, if she did not obtain more by working than was available from the welfare grant. Congresswoman Martha Griffith, Democrat of Michigan, who later headed up a subcommittee which made extensive studies of the welfare system, made perhaps the clearest and simplest statement on this issue. At hearings on the bill before the Senate Finance Committee in September 1967, she said, "This idea that you could make a choice, work or the rest of us will provide for you, is, to me, incredible." (She was later, however, to become concerned about the problem of incentives.)

Though for several years after the passage of the WIN legislation, from 1967 to 1970, we were to continue to benefit from high employment levels and a low unemployment rate, the WIN program had little impact; caseloads continued to grow in New York and throughout the country. The reasons are many. As usual, the regulations involved complex procedures, organization of the administrative bureaucracy takes time, and the level of competence is not always high. But above all there was little enthusiasm in the social welfare community or the local welfare administration for actively encouraging AFDC mothers to work—and certainly not for requiring them to do so.

It is worth noting at this point that the regulations implementing the WIN program contained elaborate safeguards for ensuring appropriate care of the child or children of the WIN mother and that various standards had to be met before the mother could be placed in training or a job. There is an Alice-in-Wonderland-ish quality to all this. In the world around us, more than half the female heads of households are working and are not on welfare. They apparently can be trusted to make adequate arrangements for the care of their children, and no official agency intervenes in the mother's decision.* But once the mother is on welfare, she cannot work unless a variety of officials agree that the child-care arrangements are satisfactory.

Commissioner Ginsberg welcomed the financial incentives

---

*There are, of course, regulatory authorities which have responsibility for ensuring the safety of group-care facilities, but not of family, friends, or baby-sitters who may care for the children or of the homes they live in.

provided in the 1967 legislation establishing the WIN program and suddenly discovered 40,000 employable heads of AFDC families on welfare, instead of his previous estimate of 8,500. But he raised a new obstacle—the fourth theme: a shortage of day-care centers. Studies done in New York City involving interviews with AFDC mothers reveal no evidence that welfare mothers regard the making of arrangements for child care a major obstacle to work.[9] They find satisfactory ways of arranging for child care after school, but the myth persists that without day-care centers, women with children cannot take jobs.

In any event, a major expansion of day-care programs was undertaken in New York and, to some extent, in other cities throughout the country. In New York City, about 42,000 children are in day-care centers or family day care, and 6,700 are in Head Start programs. Two important points may be noted. First, very few children of working welfare mothers are in the program, fewer than 2 percent in 1976–1977, a level raised to 3 percent in 1979, a minuscule advance. In fact, the program benefited mainly low middle- and middle-income families and not the welfare client. Second, the expansion was accompanied by high standards of care reflecting the view that day care should be neither just custodial care nor even early childhood programs, but childhood development programs with the emphasis on enhancing the child's capability to function through the provision of a variety of special educational, health, and counseling services. As a result, day care became very expensive—about $2,500 per year per child in the early 1970s, now closer to $3,000 per year.

The high cost of day care led to the fifth theme in the symphony of difficulties in bringing AFDC mothers into the world of work: that it was too expensive to society to have welfare mothers work. The Community Council issued a study in August 1971 which purported to prove that it would cost the taxpayers twice as much if an AFDC mother worked as if she did not; the calculation was based on adding in the cost of day care at $2,500 per year for each of two children, as well as the supplementary welfare grant which the mother needed to be paid because of the $30 and one-third disregard she was allowed as an incentive for working. The alternative of providing satisfactory but much cheaper after-school care for children of working mothers was, of course, ignored, as were the longer-term implications for economic independence.

We come finally to the sixth and last theme, a more sophisticated version of the third theme: that one could not expect the welfare mother to work if she obtained no more income than was granted to her from welfare. Now the complaint was that the marginal tax rate, 66.67 percent, was too high, a complaint heard not only from the social welfare community but from economists ranging from the conservative Milton Friedman to the moderate James Tobin.* In other words, in this view, the disregard of $30 and one-third of remaining earnings, as well as work expenses, income and social security taxes, and any costs incurred for day care, did not constitute a sufficient incentive— despite the fact that according to an analysis prepared by NYSDSS in 1977, an AFDC mother could continue to receive some supplementation from welfare until her earnings reached about $29,000 per year. Instead, attention was called to the fact that a 66.7 percent marginal tax rate was imposed by the federal income tax system only on persons with very high incomes— that is, on the portion of income exceeding well over $100,000 per year.

With the call for lower marginal tax rates on welfare clients' earnings, the trap was closed. There is no way that work at unskilled or semiskilled jobs can be made financially attractive in comparison with a reasonably decent welfare standard at an acceptable cost to society. And a drastic reduction in the welfare

---

*Indeed, Wilbur Cohen, then Secretary of Health, Education, and Welfare, and others of the social welfare community spoke up at hearings before the Senate Finance Committee in 1967 for a disregard of $50 and half the remaining earnings, as proposed in the House version of the bill under debate. During the 1977–1978 debate on the Carter proposal, Friedman again favored $50 plus half the remaining income on practical political grounds, though he feared it might not be a sufficient incentive.

standard is not an acceptable alternative. This is the rock which tore large holes in the welfare reform proposals made by President Nixon in 1969 and President Carter in 1977 and which eventually sank them.

After this review of all the reasons put forth by the liberals, the welfare community, and the welfare advocates to explain why welfare mothers couldn't or shouldn't or wouldn't work, one needs to pause to ask some questions. Does the current economy still require unskilled and semiskilled work in order to function? If the answer is yes, who should do this work? AFDC mothers and recipients of General Assistance, mainly single individuals, or somebody else? If AFDC mothers and other welfare clients, which ones? Should it be a requirement, or only voluntary? Do we need a work test, that is, the requirement to accept a definite offer of employment—private or public—and what have the results of such work tests been? Do we need government-sponsored employment programs in periods of moderate or high unemployment?

Clearly, the nature of the economy in the United States has changed over the last several decades as it has moved from a heavily industrialized to a more service-oriented economy and from a less to a far more highly technologically sophisticated economy requiring a larger proportion of very highly trained workers. But we have become so enchanted with maxi- and minicomputers, with word processing, and with adventures in space, that we sometimes forget that we all have to eat, to clothe ourselves, to use the subway or bus to get to work, and to engage in a whole variety of other activities of daily living—all of which require unskilled and semiskilled work.

We cannot buy food at the grocer's or eat in a restaurant, cafeteria, or at a luncheon counter without someone's putting the food on the shelves and marking the prices or making the sandwiches and washing the dishes. In New York City, the type of manufacturing which offered entry-level jobs to generations of immigrants in the late nineteenth century and early twentieth century, especially the apparel industry, has indeed declined, but the new mix of industry and services still offers a ratio of unskilled, semiskilled, and skilled jobs that is not too different from what prevailed in previous decades. In this connection, it may be noted that one of the fastest-growing businesses in the New York City area is the restaurant business. Further, not all the jobs related to computers are highly skilled; the computer terminal operator, for example, can be trained in a few days. Indeed, the largest occupational group in the city is clerical workers.

The peculiarities of census categories make it difficult to measure precisely the change in the ratio of the levels of skill required. According to Samuel Ehrenhalt, director of the New York Regional Office of the Bureau of Labor Statistics, however, the more significant change is that the mix is now more oriented to jobs which have traditionally been regarded as women's rather than men's jobs—that is, many are clerical office jobs.[10] This does not augur well for the young males entering the New York labor market with limited education and training, unless there is a change in traditional male and female employment patterns. But more than 90 percent of the heads of families on AFDC are women, as are about 40 percent of the single individuals on General Assistance. So, if anything, the current occupational trend should be helpful in terms of employment opportunities for the women on welfare. It is true that AFDC mothers, on the whole, are less well educated or well trained than the general female population. About 25 percent, however, have graduated from high school.

Eli Ginzberg, one of the country's leading experts on manpower (and womanpower), has estimated that 60 percent of the jobs in the regular economy are "good" jobs—that is, they pay a wage sufficient to support a family or allow advancement in the organization.[11] The other 40 percent may not be "good" jobs, but they are jobs which need to be done if the economy is to work, and, in fact, they are being done. Further, not all welfare families are four-person families; as indicated previously, about half the AFDC mothers at any point in time have only one or two children. Finally, we must recognize that the high school dropout will be limited generally to unskilled and semiskilled jobs. Society cannot afford to say that such people do not need to work, that they can choose welfare.

The 1972 amendments to the Social Security Act made it mandatory for AFDC mothers whose children are six years of age or over to register for work and accept job offers, in the absence of health problems. But a new justification arose for not enforcing the work requirement. Since the onset of the deep recession of 1974–1975, unemployment nationwide has fluctuated between 6 and 8 percent; in New York City it has remained at the high level of 8 to 9 percent, after reaching a peak of more than 11 percent in 1975–1976. In this environment, the view was commonly expressed by the welfare community, including members of the advisory committee to the HRA commissioner, that, since there was not a sufficient number of jobs to go around, enough AFDC mothers would choose to work to fill available jobs and those who did not want to work should not be coerced. A second commonly voiced opinion was this: if a welfare client (Mrs. A) were to take a job, she would only displace someone already working or just about to get that job (Mrs. B), and all that would happen is that Mrs. B would replace Mrs. A on welfare.

Apart from the spurious economic analysis, which viewed the labor market as utterly rigid with some fixed number of jobs available, this view completely ignored the attitude of the general public in a society in which 60 percent of married women with school-age children are working, many at jobs paying the minimum wage or only modest wages. Such workers regard it as incomprehensible, unjust, and even outrageous that a part of the population should be permitted to choose welfare over work if the price is not right. Here is an illustration of the lack of logic in the thinking of the social welfare community on this issue: in 1978, I announced to the advisory committee that we were going to offer jobs at the minimum wage in HRA's expanding Home Attendant Program to both AFDC mothers and single women on General Assistance. The announcement was greeted with dismay and disapproval. Here was a service which they all regarded highly—assistance to the aged or disabled to make it possible for them to continue living in their own homes with proper care. But they wanted other people to take these jobs, not women on welfare.*

This opposition to a work requirement, if it meant minimum or modest wages, also ignored what was happening with respect to illegal immigration into the city and the surrounding area during the 1970s. We know far too little about the magnitude or characteristics of illegal immigration to the area, but we do know that the volume is significant and that very few of these people are on welfare. The illegal immigrants are working; many find work within days after their arrival in the city. And they have no difficulty borrowing social security cards from family and friends to show the employer. It is probable that many, though not all, are working at minimum wage jobs, and many, because of their illegal status, are undoubtedly exploited and denied the prevailing wage for the job or the fringe benefits which they should receive. But they are performing a vital economic function in the city; some are undoubtedly working as home attendants aiding the aged and disabled. They are filling jobs which welfare recipients will not take because it is not "worthwhile."

DO WE NEED A WORK TEST?

Obviously, unemployment rates of 7 to 9 percent have an adverse impact on the ability of welfare clients to find jobs, but too much evidence is available to indicate that a significant number of jobs—jobs which are essential to the economy—can be obtained and filled by welfare clients. There is also considerable evidence to indicate the need for a work test to ensure that all those who can work—not to mention those working off

---

*In fact, the complexities of WIN are such that it turned out to be impossible to refer AFDC mothers to these jobs. Subsequently, efforts were undertaken by HRA, however, to train welfare clients on general assistance to be home attendants, but training is limited to single individuals.

the books and not reporting their income to the welfare authorities—do take available jobs.

Since July 1971, when employable welfare recipients in New
York State were required to pick up their checks at the NYSES
office and register for employment, data have indicated not only
that some do not pick up their checks but that at each stage of
the process—referral to a job, appearance for the interview, and
acceptance of a job offer—some number drop off and their cases
can be closed. As indicated previously, in the early months of
the program as many as 20 percent of employable clients did
not pick up their checks. The rate had to settle down, of course.
Nevertheless, in January 1980, as many as 7.2 percent were
sanctioned for failing to comply with one or more steps of the
procedure. One can reasonably assume that such clients have
other sources of income.

Equally revealing are the results of the work test in the form
of what is generally referred to as "workfare" but has various
names in different states. In New York it is called the Public
Works Program (PWP), a program which involves working off
the welfare grant at prevailing wages in various jobs in state
and city agencies and, to some extent, in nonprofit agencies. (It
can be used, however, only with respect to General Assistance
cases. The WIN program pre-empts the work test for AFDC
clients.) In New York City, where beginning in 1977 HRA succeeded in substantially enlarging PWP employment, it was found
that of the total number referred for jobs, 13 percent failed to
report for a PWP interview, 5 percent refused to accept an assignment, and 4 percent accepted the assignment but failed to
report for work—a total of 21 percent whose cases were closed,
of which about half remained closed for six months or more.
The offer of full-time CETA jobs paying better than $7,500 per
year to mainly single welfare recipients in the city resulted in a
refusal rate of about 40 percent—a startling figure. Another effort involved the assignment of NYSES personnel with access to
the central NYSES computer bank at a welfare center serving
mainly General Assistance cases. In the first three months of
1980, a total of 518 persons were called in for interviews and

referrals to jobs; 196, or 36 percent, failed to respond. If the usual ratio holds, about half the cases closed because of failure to comply will remain closed.

What emerges in a review of work programs in New York and in other states which have such programs is that work programs are more expensive on a one-for-one basis than a cash-grant program. Not only must some allowance be provided for work expenses, but the costs of administering a work program are substantial, especially when account is taken of supervision, supplies, and materials necessary to perform the work. On the other hand, a great deal of useful work is done by welfare recipients assigned to work programs. Indeed, many agencies in the city, including HRA, would find it difficult to perform their functions without the PWP workers assigned to them. The same is, of course, equally true of CETA jobs. But the work test requiring General Assistance recipients, who are mainly single individuals without children, to work off their grants uncovers a significant percentage who must have other resources, probably from work, who therefore refuse the assignment and whose cases are closed. The savings in welfare costs are substantial.

A fascinating fact is that offers of full-time CETA jobs, which pay an average of $7,500 per year, or of jobs in private employment which pay a minimum of $5,600 per year for a thirty-five-hour week (both figures are more than double the cash welfare grant for a single individual) elicit a refusal rate almost double the rate for part-time jobs. Apparently, part-time workfare jobs can be fitted into other paid employment not reported to the welfare administration, but full-time offers of employment cannot.

Because of the restrictions imposed by the legislation establishing the WIN program and the federal regulations which implement it, workfare programs such as PWP cannot be applied to an AFDC mother.* Whether a refusal rate as high as 21 percent would also be obtained among employable AFDC recip-

*The changes in the 1981 amendments which affect work requirements for AFDC mothers are described later in this chapter.

ients cannot be foretold. Some limited experience with offers of temporary full-time employment in entry-level jobs paying about $7,000 per year in HRA itself apparently revealed a refusal rate of about 15 percent, but the number of jobs involved was small and the results were subject to some interpretation. The effort revealed one interesting fact, however; of the thirty-three women called in for the jobs, only one could not accept the offer because of a child-care problem.

Should welfare mothers be required to work at available jobs paying at least minimum wages and meeting other legal requirements? In my view, program integrity, equity, and increased potential for long-term independence require an affirmative answer. It is encouraging to note that this view is now shared by at least a majority of current welfare administrators throughout the country, as evidenced by a March 1981 report issued by the Employment Committee of the American Public Welfare Association (APWA) and endorsed by its board of directors. They urge that "income assistance for those individuals who are employable (essentially all adults not eligible under SSI categories and who are in need of income support) should serve as a 'back-up' to employment rather than as an alternative to employment" and that exemptions from a requirement to accept available employment should cover only the single head of a household when the youngest child is under three years of age. Such a statement from APWA would have been unheard of during the sixties and seventies.

The opposite view, which prevailed in the sixties and seventies in New York and other urban areas, was that few AFDC mothers were employable or, if they were, that they should not be required to take "menial" jobs, that they should receive a financial incentive to work and at a low marginal tax rate, or that it is too expensive to taxpayers to make mothers with children work. The ideological justification for this view is simply not in accord with the facts, the economic requirements of the society, or the general sense of equity or fairness. It is not acceptable for some to decide that they would rather not work and that it's all right because enough people seem to want to work and will produce enough to support them. As former Congress-woman Martha Griffiths said, it is an "incredible notion."

The 1980 elections not only brought Ronald Reagan to the White House and a Republican majority to the Senate but also brought a different set of attitudes toward welfare and work and the political will and acumen to effect significant change. How far has it gone?

THE REAGAN SEA CHANGE—OR IS IT?

Reagan came out of California proud of his accomplish-ments in reducing the state's welfare caseload and raising its welfare grants and irritated by federal policies and regulations which limited the actions a governor was permitted to take with respect to workfare programs and other detailed provisions af-fecting eligibility and benefit levels. His experience and views are clearly reflected in the series of recommendations he sub-mitted to Congress on the AFDC program, recommendations adopted in the main in the budget reconciliation process. These may be analyzed within the framework of the three major is-sues—the level of ineligibility and overpayments, the level of the welfare grant, and incentives to work—to see the extent of change and to judge whether they have gone so far as to impose serious injury on recipients or potential applicants.

The major new tools for reducing ineligibility and overpay-ments in the 1981 amendments are retrospective budgeting and monthly reporting. The former requires that eligibility be deter-mined on the basis of income and resources at the time of application and that benefit levels be based on income and re-sources during the preceding month, except for the first month of assistance.* This system ties in with the second requirement,

---

*This exception is important, as it avoids the pitfall of denying aid to a family which had income last month but not this month—that is, the month in which application for welfare is being made. Unfortunately, the same procedure was not followed with respect to the food stamp program. See chapter 4.

that welfare recipients file a monthly report on their earnings and other income as well as any change in assets. This report then serves as the basis for determining the benefit level in the following month. The proponents of the procedure anticipate that the combination of retrospective budgeting and monthly reporting will uncover in a more timely fashion those who have become ineligible, or those whose benefits should be reduced because of increased income from other sources.

The retrospective budgeting feature was to become effective as of October 1, 1981, but the goal was unrealistic since inadequate time was allowed for drafting of new procedures and training local staff. New York State has requested a waiver of the provision but as of January 1982 has not yet had a response. Other states have also asked for waivers. But the more important observations to be made are that the monthly reports cannot be handled without a massive increase in existing computer capability at state and local levels, and that this will take many, many months, if not several years, to accomplish. Further, it is moot whether monthly reporting is more effective than the simpler and less expensive mail-outs every three or four months.* In any event, no savings are anticipated during fiscal 1982. Indeed substantial costs will be incurred for the additional computer technology.

HRA has proposed to mount a pilot project beginning February 1, 1982, in two income maintenance centers in the city limited to families on AFDC or GA, as well as single persons on General Assistance, who are employed or obtaining unemployment insurance. Simultaneously, the monthly reporting system would be tested for these same groups of recipients. If the pilot test runs smoothly, the system will be extended to all income maintenance centers in the city about August 1, 1982, but only for the limited groups noted. HRA has also expressed a willingness to try retrospective budgeting and monthly reporting for

---

*The states are permitted to request an exemption from the monthly reporting requirement for certain groups of clients if they can show that the monthly report would not be cost-effective.

the entire caseload in one income maintenance center. It too would not begin until the summer of 1982. Whether either pilot test is undertaken depends on the federal response to the request for a waiver.

The savings estimated from the different amendments passed in 1981 are shown in the tabulation on page 54.[12]

A reduction in overpayments in fiscal 1982 is expected to result from new provisions requiring prompt repayment by the client of any overpayments received, regardless of any hardships this may impose on the client. The monthly deduction of the repayment, however, cannot be so large that the client is left with a sum equal to less than 90 percent of the standard of need. It is the "hardship" provision, rather ill-defined in the previous legislation, which had constituted the loophole permitting clients to avoid repaying excess welfare benefits in a significant number of cases.

The 1981 amendments do not deal directly with the issue of the level of the welfare standard. The right of each state to determine its standard of need is maintained, as is the requirement that the standard be applied uniformly throughout the state. (The "standard of need" is the sum which will be granted to a family without any other source of income. The benefit level equals the standard of need minus income from earnings or other sources, such as unemployment insurance, plus allowable deductions.) For the future, however, states will be permitted to consider as available income the value of the family's food stamp allotment or any rent or housing subsidy to the extent that such a subsidy duplicates allowances in the standard of need. Thus some recognition is given in federal law governing welfare payments to the existence of other federal benefits which constitute part of the welfare package. But since many states had already recognized the connection within the last few years, at least with respect to food stamps, no significant amount of savings will result from this provision.

The new amendments will, however, have a significant impact on the determination of eligibility and on benefit levels, as a result of a number of changes in the definition of who is eli-

Estimated Federal Savings from 1981 Amendments in Fiscal 1982

	AMOUNT (millions of dollars)	PERCENT
Level of ineligibility and overpayments	115	21.1
Retrospective budgeting and monthly reporting	0	—
Adjustments for overpayments	115	21.1
Level of welfare grant	10	1.8
Counting food stamp benefits	10	1.8
Level of welfare benefits	269	49.3
Resource limit reduced to $1,000	16	2.9
Lump sum payments	5	.9
Earned income tax credit (EITC)	19	3.5
Stepparent income	154	28.1
Dependent child (under eighteen)	50	9.2
Pregnant women (third trimester)	20	3.7
Strikers	5	.9
Incentives to work	137	25.1
Earned income disregard (EID)	75	13.7
Four-month limit on EID	62	11.4
Income limit (150 percent of welfare standard)	0	—
Work programs	0	—
Community Work Experience program	0	—
Work Supplementation program	0	—
Work Incentive (WIN) demonstration program	0	—
Other	15	2.7
Sponsor responsibility for aliens	15	2.7
Payments below $10 per month	0	—
Elimination of 20 percent limit on vendor-restricted checks	0	—
Total	546	100.0

gible for AFDC, the allowable level of resources, and categories of income which can no longer be excluded from consideration in calculating benefit levels. These changes are as follows:

1. The allowable limitation on assets is reduced from $1,500 to $1,000, and exclusions are limited to an owner-occupied house, one automobile (if valued at or below the amount set by the Secretary of Health and Human Services),* and ordinary household furnishings. Further, income and assets of any child or other relative or individual in the home are to be taken into account in determining eligibility; previously, part-time earnings of children under eighteen were disregarded. If the family is eligible, however, children's part-time earnings will continue to be disregarded in calculating family benefits, in order to encourage them to seek part-time employment.

2. If the family receives a lump sum payment, such as a settlement of an injury claim, it becomes ineligible for the number of months equal to the payment divided by the standard of need, but it remains eligible for Medicaid.

3. In families with an earner, the estimated earned income tax credit (EITC) is assumed as monthly income even though it is not received on a monthly basis. This provision is designed to avoid the situation in which EITC, received in a lump sum, is quickly spent and no longer available to offset the welfare benefit.

4. States are required to take into account a stepparent's income to the extent that it exceeds the total of $75 for work expenses, plus the standard of need for himself and any of his dependents living in the household, plus other payments the stepparent may be making for alimony, child support, or support of other dependents

---

*This provision is clearly directed at states which might want to be too generous—and is somewhat in conflict with the new federalism, which ordinarily would leave decisions on such minor details to the states.

living outside the household. Previously, a stepparent had no responsibility to support his stepchildren; this provision accounts for one of the larger savings in the list.

5. A dependent child is defined as a child under the age of eighteen unless he or she is completing high school in the nineteenth year. The previous definition also included children up to age twenty-one, if they were attending an institution of higher learning.

6. AFDC payments to pregnant women are restricted to the third trimester instead of beginning in the first, and such coverage has been made an option of the state. Medicaid coverage remains available, however, as soon as pregnancy is confirmed.

7. Participation in a strike is no longer considered good cause for leaving or refusing to accept employment, and AFDC payments are prohibited to the whole family if the caretaker relative is on strike. If another family member is on strike, his or her needs are not provided for in the family grant.

Among the seven changes noted above, the first three, the reduction in allowable assets, the handling of lump sum payments, and the provisions regarding EITC result in relatively small savings, about $40 million of federal funds and a slightly lower amount of state and local costs. They are obviously less generous to clients but cannot be regarded as unreasonable. Handling the EITC as if it were received monthly will, however, create considerable administrative difficulty and put a squeeze on families who do not have that $1,000 in resources to utilize, or cannot borrow from friends and relatives until the EITC is actually paid to them.

The inclusion of part-time earnings of children under eighteen raises an interesting question. The previous exclusion of such earnings was based on the judgment that if one wanted to encourage youngsters to work, one had to let them keep all their earnings for their own personal use and could not obligate them to use all or part of their earnings to contribute to the support of the family, thereby decreasing the amount needed for welfare.* A modification of this view prevailed in the 1981 amendment. If a youngster's earnings raise family income to 150 percent or more of the state standard of need, the family will not be eligible for welfare. If, however, family income does not reach the 150 percent level and the family becomes eligible for some welfare benefits, the youngster's earnings are disregarded, since there is no way to impose a work test on the youngster. Thus the youngster's obligation to the family and, in a sense, to society is stressed, but recognition is also given to administrative practicalities.

Policy regarding a stepparent's responsibility for stepchildren has also reflected divergent views on family responsibility and on how the stepparent would react to the obligation to provide support. The social welfare community assumed that the imposition of the obligation to support would discourage a man from marrying a mother on AFDC. There was little analytical evidence for this view. After all, over the decades, many marriages have taken place between men and widows with children, and the stepfather, as a matter of course, has supported the children of the previous marriage within the limits of his financial ability. Nevertheless, the view was firmly held for many years and was imbedded in the Social Security Act.** The 1981 change recognizes a traditional view of family responsibility and obligation. The change accounts for 28 percent of the total savings in federal funds anticipated for fiscal 1982; it is the largest single source of savings. It would be interesting if someone did a study to see whether the new provision regarding stepparent responsibility has any effect on the remarriage rate of low-income women.

*Some also regarded this as a good way of providing some extra money to the family over and above the welfare standard.
**Only in April 1981 did APWA's National Council of State Administrators come to agree with the Reagan administration's proposal to take account of stepparent income. See American Public Welfare Association, *Washington Report* 16, no. 3 (April 1981): 7.

The amendments which exclude eighteen- to twenty-one-year-olds attending college, limit aid to pregnant women to the third trimester, and exclude strikers' families from benefits cannot be regarded as benign. Further, while they will save federal funds, about $75 million, or 14 percent of total estimated savings, the burden will, in the main, only be transferred to the states and localities, which have General Assistance programs for families and single persons. New York will be especially hard hit. The elimination of strikers' families is especially harsh, taken in conjunction with the disqualification of strikers from eligibility for food stamps. (See chapter 4 for a discussion of rules affecting strikers' eligibility for food stamps.) In New York, however, strikers and their families will be eligible under the General Assistance program.

The major conceptual change embodied in the 1981 amendments is that the whole notion of providing welfare clients with a financial incentive to work, first introduced into the public assistance program in 1967, has been thrown right out the window. First, the earning disregard is substantially reduced; work expenses are standardized and include the first $75 per month of earned income and up to $160 per month per child for day care in the case of a parent employed full time for the entire month. Second, though a further earnings disregard of $30 and a third of remaining income (in place of gross income) is permitted, this disregard is available only for the first four consecutive months of employment, and it cannot be applied again until twelve consecutive months have passed. In sum, an allowance for work expenses and child care is granted indefinitely so that the welfare client will not be worse off when working than when on welfare. It must be said, however, that $75 per month, the figure set for such expenses, may prove too low in New York and other major cities, where subways and buses cost 75 cents or more per ride, and even a brown-bagged lunch can cost well over a dollar. But beyond the first four months, no additional cash incentive is provided. The whole debate about marginal tax rates has been terminated, and we have returned to the notion that those who can work should work.

In sum, 77 percent of the cuts which will be effective in fiscal 1982 reflect reasonable changes in legislative policies. About 14 percent will prove harsh except in states such as New York where the clients involved may be picked up under the General Assistance program, and about 9 percent may be regarded as less generous, or inconvenient, or, in the case of holding sponsors responsible for aliens, probably unenforceable in the courts.

Obviously, I support the elimination of the financial incentive and its replacement by an obligation on the part of the welfare client to work, assuming the absence of young children and disabling health problems. But this obligation, like the obligation to pay taxes, must be enforceable. By "enforceable," I mean that either employment opportunities in the private sector must be widely available or public service jobs must fill the gap. We need to examine the remaining amendments which relate to WIN and other work programs to determine whether realistic provision has been made.

Two major changes have been wrought by the 1981 amendments, and again these are changes in concept. First, AFDC mothers will no longer be exempt from workfare programs, as they have been since 1967. Under a new Community Work Experience Program (CWEP), AFDC mothers may be required to work at public service jobs for a maximum number of hours per month; the number of hours is equal to the value of the AFDC benefit plus the food stamp allotment divided by the minimum wage.* Reasonable necessary costs for transportation and other expenses are to be provided. Second, employable AFDC mothers whose children are three years of age or over are required to participate in workfare programs if adequate child care is available (previously, mothers with children under six years were not required to work).

---

*The requirement for use of the minimum instead of the prevailing wage is a bad decision, in my view. It will arouse a sense of injustice among welfare clients doing the same work as regular employees who are being paid the prevailing wage and will exacerbate union opposition to workfare programs.

Some limitation on the potentialities of CWEP as a work experience and a work test must, however, be noted. The program is to be instituted at the option of each state, and the decision for or against exercising the option will be influenced by the politics of welfare at the state level. One can anticipate a loud and sustained chorus from the social welfare leaders in New York and other states opposing it as "slave labor," as they have opposed similar programs in the past. Further, while the federal government will share in the costs incurred by clients for transportation and other necessary work expenses, the federal agencies will not share the cost of materials, equipment, and supervision. This prohibition may act as a brake on states that would otherwise wish to opt for CWEP, as such administrative costs are substantial. Even if states do opt for the program, they may not do so on the large scale necessary to make it effective as a work experience and a work test. State and local budget directors operating under heavy fiscal constraints are not always easily persuaded to authorize outlays of hard cash in one period for anticipated savings in the next. The prohibition seems a foolish penny-pinching device, since the federal government will receive half the benefit of the reduction in AFDC costs after fiscal 1982; past experience with workfare programs for the general assistance caseload indicates that savings will be realized.

States will also have the option under the 1981 amendments of establishing a Work Supplementation program and a Work Incentive (WIN) demonstration program. Under the former, all or part of the wages of a specified job may be paid out of AFDC funds; under the latter, various demonstration programs can be undertaken relating to job training, job finding clubs, diversion of the welfare grant to public or private sector employers to be included in the wages paid, service contracts with state employment services or CETA prime sponsors, private placement agencies, and so on. The programs do indeed constitute a varied arsenal, but each element involves elaborate administrative mechanisms, and the programs are unlikely to be implemented with great speed or on a large scale.

Finally the basic WIN program remains in place, minus the financial incentive; it requires employable AFDC mothers whose children are over three years of age to register for employment and to accept a job if one is offered. Whether this requirement will be more effective in the future than it has been in the past will depend, in part, on whether the state employment services will play a more active role in finding jobs for AFDC clients. In New York and in other states, the state employment service has been mainly concerned with maintaining its reputation as a good source for employers to turn to for finding labor. As a result, it has been restrained, to say the least, in its efforts to make job referrals for welfare clients who are often inadequately trained, lack work discipline, and may be unenthusiastic about accepting job offers. But, in part, the effectiveness of WIN will also depend on the general level of unemployment. If unemployment remains at over 7 percent nationally, at 8 to 9 percent in New York City, and at even higher levels in many other cities, the prospects are less than bright.

How do all the changes add up? First, in dollar terms, it has been estimated by both the Executive Office and the Congressional Budget Office (CBO) that expenditures for benefit payments to AFDC recipients will reach $13.1 billion in fiscal 1981 and will rise to $14.3 or $14.4 billion in fiscal 1982. The federal savings the CBO anticipates in fiscal 1982 from the Reagan amendments equal $546 million. Adding in state and local savings brings the figure to just over $1 billion, or about 7 percent of previously estimated benefit payments for the year. So this is not, in its magnitude, a sea change.

Of the nineteen separate changes affecting benefits, four are significant in their impact, each accounting for 10 percent or more of the total. In order of importance, they are (1) inclusion of stepparent income (28.1 percent), (2) adjustments for overpayments (21.1 percent), (3) the reduction in the earned income disregard (13.7 percent), and (4) the four-month limitation on the disregard of $30 and one-third of remaining earnings (11.4 percent). These changes, along with the new work programs, which are not expected to realize savings in the first year, do reflect something of a sea change—a shift back to more traditional attitudes of family responsibility to share income and the head of the family's responsibility to work and a more rigorous adherence to whatever standard of need the state establishes. In the new climate there will be some further reduction in ineligibility and overpayments and some decline in caseloads as welfare clients who have been working or begin to work exhaust the four-month earnings disregard and as others in the "underground" economy refuse workfare or other job offers. But the decline will not be large. Much more must be done to achieve a substantial reduction in long-term dependency, especially among blacks and other minority groups—a subject which is left for the last chapter of this book.

CHAPTER 3

Shouldn't Low-Income Fathers Support Their Children?

The title of this chapter may seem odd. If there is any proposition which would receive an extraordinarily high affirmative vote in a national poll, it is that parents are responsible for the care and support of their children if they are physically, mentally, and financially able to do so. In particular, the father is regarded as having this obligation, whether he is present in the house or not. It is a principle embedded in national and state laws governing domestic relations. And yet there has always been some gap between principle and reality, and the gap has widened in recent decades as divorce rates have skyrocketed and the number of children born out of wedlock has risen with each passing year.

While many divorces are accompanied by amicable agreements relating to financial support, many are bitterly fought through the courts. In cases of dispute, the decision on the amount of the support payment lies with the individual judge, who is given little more than general guidance in law or custom as to what the just or reasonable amount should be. The result is enormous variation in the value of support orders imposed on fathers with the same income and financial worth and/or with the same family circumstances, if they have remarried. Further, as time passes, it is not uncommon for payments to become irregular or erratic and sometimes to cease, requiring further recourse to the courts—an expensive, time-consuming, and traumatic process.

Anecdotal material indicates that some fathers with middle- or upper-level incomes fail to provide any support or sufficient support and so force the wife and children to apply for public assistance. But the data available from various sources on the income and occupations of the "absent" fathers of AFDC families do not indicate that this situation is at all widespread. The sense of obligation of the divorced or otherwise absent father to support his family holds, by and large, in the middle- and upper-income groups, or else the family obtains support from sources other than public assistance.

The sense of obligation of the low- or relatively low-income father has greatly weakened, as evidenced by the huge increase during the last two decades in the number of female-headed families on welfare, most of them receiving no financial support from the absent fathers. Indeed, to the extent that it provides an alternative, the welfare system itself may, in significant measure, be responsible for the diminished sense of obligation felt by low-income fathers to support their children. One Family Court judge recounted to me a typical case in her court in which she asked the father how much financial support he was giving to his wife and children; he replied, "She doesn't need help from me. She's on welfare." One must ask how such an attitude, so contrary to both the ideal and the norm, developed and became widespread. Are such attitudes and the resulting behavior acceptable to society as a whole? And, if not, can they be changed, and by what means?

This chapter is an attempt to respond to these questions. It will recount efforts by Congress and state legislatures to deal with the problem of nonsupport, and it will examine how these efforts were received by those who influenced or were responsible for the state and local administration of welfare and child support programs. In particular, it will assay the roles of the liberal social welfare community and the Family Court judges. The former influences the ambiance for implementation of the policy—in this case, unfavorably. The latter have an enormous influence on efforts to institute appropriate administrative techniques to implement the program effectively. As with most welfare programs, administration has as much impact, if not more, on the results as does the statement of policy.

THE LEGISLATIVE BACKGROUND

When the AFDC program was first established in the Social Security Act of 1935, relatively little attention was paid to the issue of child support payments. The presumption was that most recipients would be widows with children or the wives and children of disabled fathers, and this was in fact the case during the early years of the program. The change started in the 1950s and accelerated through the next two decades. In 1980, in the country as a whole, only about 4 percent of the fathers of AFDC recipients were deceased or disabled; in New York City, fewer than 2 percent were. But while the characteristics of the welfare caseload changed, and although most state laws provided that support should be sought from the absent fathers, few steps were taken by state or local welfare administrations to mount any serious effort to accomplish this purpose. One reason is that the facts had not yet caught up with the presumption. Another, as this chapter will relate, is that such efforts were not welcomed by the social welfare community or the judiciary.

In 1950, federal legislation for the first time required that prompt notice be furnished to law enforcement officials when AFDC was granted as a result of desertion or abandonment, but this requirement had little effect.[1] Stronger measures were taken in 1967, when Congress required states to establish a formal program to secure child support. The effectiveness of such efforts varied from state to state; New York was not among the successful states—quite the contrary. A review by the General Accounting Office (GAO) attributed the uneven performance of the various states to the failure of the Department of Health, Education, and Welfare to monitor the state programs and require statistical reporting, but later experience indicates that was not the only, or even the major, reason.

Dissatisfaction with the ineffectiveness of the 1967 amendments led Congress to require a more determined effort by federal, state, and local welfare administrators to secure an effective system for obtaining child support. The result was the passage in 1974 of Title IV-D of the Social Security Act. In reporting out the bill, the Senate Committee on Finance stated: "The Committee believes that all children should have the right to receive support from their fathers. The Committee bill is designed to help children attain this right, including the right to have their fathers identified so that support can be obtained. The immediate result will be a lower welfare cost to the taxpayer but, more importantly, as an effective support collection system is established fathers will be deterred from deserting their families to welfare and children will be spared the effects of family breakup."[2]

Title IV-D, which came into effect August 1, 1975, requires as a condition of eligibility for AFDC that every applicant or recipient assign support rights to the state and cooperate with the state in establishing paternity and securing child support.* In return for the welfare client's assignment of support rights, the state is to provide a full welfare grant to the recipient. The main purpose of this latter provision is to spare the AFDC mother the hardship of erratic support payments and assure her the steady income of the welfare grant. The support payments obtained from the absent father are retained by the welfare administration, and the net receipts are divided among the federal, state, and local governments according to a legislatively determined formula.

Title IV-D also laid down a number of requirements for HEW, the Internal Revenue Service, and the states with respect

---

*In this context, "state" includes the political subdivisions of the state as well.

to the administration of the program, all designed to promote an aggressive, effective administration of the law. It provided for 75 percent federal reimbursement of the costs, instead of the usual 50 percent. And as a further incentive, it permitted the state or locality to keep 25 percent of total collections for a year and 15 percent thereafter, in addition to its usual 25 percent share. (The extra 25 or 15 percent comes out of the federal share of income support payments obtained.) In sum, after two decades of benign neglect of the child support issue, Congress moved in a massive way to create a system to maximize efforts to obtain support from absent fathers of AFDC recipients.

As with any new large-scale program, establishing the administrative mechanisms was difficult and time-consuming; this program was particularly complex. Not only did HEW have the usual regulatory and monitoring responsibilities, but it also had certain operational duties, such as the establishment of a parent locator system. As problems arose, recrimination was rife among the federal agencies, the states, and the localities; each accused the others of not doing what they were supposed to do. In addition, the close cooperation of the Family Court was required. In states such as New York, which have state-supervised, locally administered welfare systems, the local agency had to reorganize staff and gear up to operate the program. In New York City, initiation of the IV-D program coincided with the beginning of the acute phase of the city's fiscal crisis. Massive layoffs occurred in the Human Resources Administration, as in other agencies; seniority rules required transfer of large numbers of staff members into different jobs; and the unions did not make life any easier by prolonged negotiations over the appropriate duties of staff in various positions.

Despite all the problems, common in other states as well as in New York, the program not only got under way but, by the end of 1976, the first full year of operation, collections exceeded expenditures in most states and in New York State, except for New York City. Philip Toia, Commissioner of Social Services at this time, in submitting the annual report on the program to the governor and the legislature wrote as follows: "Perhaps the most important conclusion that should be drawn from our experience to date is this: IV-D can work. It may seem surprising that this is being presented as a conclusion two years after Congress mandated the program. Yet in many ways, the conclusion is an appropriate one. For probably no other major initiative in the field of public welfare has in recent years been as controversial as IV-D. No other program has been as widely attacked by professionals in the field as misconceived, misdirected, and doomed to failure."

The Attitudes and Impact of the Social Welfare Community

Nowhere was the attack against the program by the social welfare community more acute and more sustained than in New York City. The Community Council of Greater New York, a coordinating group for many of the social welfare organizations in the city, began to monitor the program in February 1976. An interim report issued at the end of the year was appropriately critical of many aspects of the administration of the program. But what is revealing is that one looks in vain in the report for some affirmation of the notion that fathers have an obligation to support their children, if they are able to do so. One finds instead that the purposes of the report were to determine (1) the program's impact on AFDC families, especially young children, (2) whether the client's civil rights were affected through authorized procedures, (3) whether the program "would contribute a further harassment of AFDC recipients and their families," and, finally, (4) "whether its costs would outweigh revenues collected."

The final report, entitled *Who Should Support the Children?* and issued in spring 1978, again made some serious criticism of HRA's administration of the program. For example, it said that "support and paternity cases are poorly prepared by the Department of Social Services (DSS) for Family Court and representation in Family Court has been inadequate"—all too true. It also pointed out that "cases move slowly and poorly through the Family Court. Collection measures have, until recently, been at best, haphazard or nonexistent, almost permitting the non-payment of support and the accumulation of arrears. There has been little if any successful enforcement of support orders." Again, all too true. But HRA rejected as unfounded the charge that efforts to obtain information on the absent father's where-abouts from the AFDC applicant constituted harassment and resulted in unfair rejection of applications.[3]

When it came to its policy statement, however, the Community Council was ambiguous, at best, and, at worst, basically hostile to an aggressive program to obtain child support from absent fathers. It attributed the increased federal role in collecting support payments—a development it deplored—to the increased costs to the federal government resulting from the rapid increase in welfare caseloads during the sixties. It did not accept the congressional view that the problem was due to the nonsupport of children by absent parents. Rather, it asserted, "Concerns about AFDC fiscal solvency many times masked intense hostility toward the recipients of the program, hostility toward their race, their sex and their poverty."

In following its "own philosophical disposition in order to establish a conceptual framework consistent with [its] beliefs" for dealing with the issues of who should support children and the rights of families on public assistance, the Community Council questioned the general societal disposition to place a high value on marriage and pointed to the increase in the number of female-headed families in the United States during the last two decades. It rejected the findings of any studies which point to a connection between welfare and family break-up, real or collusive; it questioned whether the absent fathers had sufficient income to support their families and, without data, or in disregard of existing data, it answered the question in the negative. It expressed doubt that it would be possible to establish paternity for the large number of out-of-wedlock children, though, as the report itself indicates, establishing paternity proved to be relatively easy;* and it concluded that the child support program would work effectively only where a legal marriage existed, paternity had been established, the father's whereabouts were known, and his income was adequate to contribute toward his dependents.

This was a curious indictment; the purpose of the law was, among other things, to promote efforts to establish paternity for those children who needed to have it established—those born out of wedlock—and to locate the fathers, recognizing that this would indeed take some effort. Perhaps the Council's view was most clearly expressed in the paragraph which stated: "The Child Support Enforcement [IV-D] legislation as promulgated has serious flaws. It has failed to deal with the need of children for an adequate home and, by stressing the primary role of the absent parent, fails to deal with the role that the government should play in guaranteeing an adequate income for families. We believe that that right should be made distinct through a guaranteed minimum income for children and families."

Apart from the Community Council, many social welfare leaders in the community—who were, at various times between 1975 and 1979, members of the advisory committee to the HRA commissioner—opposed the program as reflected in the written minutes of the meetings. They urged James Dumpson (commissioner in 1975–1976), J. Henry Smith (1976–1977), and me (1978–1979) to oppose it. As early as January 30, 1975, most of the members of the advisory board (then called the Resources Re-

---

*The report stated: "In the paternity cases observed monitors noted that the alleged fathers were readily willing to acknowledge paternity even after a lengthy explanation by the judges that such an acknowledgment would entail an obligation to support the child until the age of majority, even in those cases where the statute of limitations had expired. In fact, in many cases it appeared almost a matter of pride for the man to acknowledge paternity. Moreover, the men in the paternity cases observed appeared willing to provide support to the best of their ability" (p. 64). I made a similar observation with respect to acknowledgment of paternity in a visit I paid to the Brooklyn Family Court in 1978, but had a different view with respect to support payments (this visit is discussed later in this chapter).

view Board) expressed the view that "the concept had been proven to be not worthwhile on a cost-benefit basis in the past." At a June 30, 1975, meeting, Commissioner Dumpson presented data obtained from NYSDSS indicating that location and support efforts preceding the IV-D program had indeed been effective. Committee members expressed disbelief. Meeting with Commissioner Smith on September 13, 1976, members argued that "conditions in New York City are not propitious for finding fathers and once found, getting them to pay is difficult."

Though some changes in membership had occurred by the time I became HRA commissioner, the general attitude of the advisory committee had not. At my first meeting with the committee, I informed them that I was convinced the program could work well in the city if state and city officials took appropriate actions within their spheres of responsibility and made a common approach to the Family Court to achieve improvement on a range of matters dealing with the processing of cases and the amount of court support orders. The response of some committee members was that I ought to tell the state commissioner that I would make an "honest effort" to reach the goal but that an "honest look at the program may reveal that it is not possible to make it cost-effective." I declined, since in my view the problem was that the IV-D program started in New York City with a staff convinced that it was not ever going to be cost-effective and the advisory committee bore a large degree of responsibility for that attitude.

There were clear indications of the impact of the advisory committee's attitude on the operation of the program. By August 1976, a year after its initiation, the program in New York City was, in the view of NYSDSS, in complete disarray. HEW officials were threatening sanctions against the state—sanctions which could have meant heavy financial penalties the state and city could ill afford.* Commissioner Toia wrote Commissioner Smith a letter that was sharp in tone and lengthy in its indict-

---

*These threats continued through most of 1977. In the end, however, they were avoided, as HRA was able to claim sufficient improvement in 1978 over the situation found by audits in 1976 and 1977.

ment; it can be summarized in one sentence: "The examination of New York City's IV-D program has revealed grave deficiencies in all areas of the child support effort."

At a subsequent meeting of top officials in NYSDSS and HRA, what was particularly disturbing to state officials was Commissioner Smith's comment that "the philosophy of the program seems good but the practicality is terrible. I don't know if it will ever be a good program. I had a meeting with my Advisory Committee today—these are the high priests of welfare—and they don't believe the program is good or can be. Conditions in New York City . . . make it impossible. Motivations are all wrong; to assume it will do the job it's supposed to do is probably a mirage." One state official responded by admitting that the national goals for IV-D might be hard to achieve in New York City, but added that if city officials started out by saying that the program was fundamentally no good, that view would be communicated to other city agencies involved and would become a self-fulfilling prophecy. But Commissioner Smith went on even more strongly, saying, "This program is anathema from the point of view of welfare workers and is an impossibility as far as accomplishment is concerned. It's an anathema in the view of clients; when the wife gets her money, she doesn't care if it's from her husband or the state. It's a mixed bag and we should face up to facts that would tend to make this a self-fulfilling prophecy."

As one reviews these expressions of opposition on the part of the social welfare community, including its "high priests," to the efforts to obtain child support from absent fathers, the following major justifications for the position emerge:

1. The children may be endangered, or the mothers may be harassed and their civil rights abridged.
2. The notion that the father should ordinarily be regarded as the primary source of support for the children is outdated and to be superseded by the view that government must guarantee an adequate income for people for whatever life style they choose to follow.
3. The fathers can't be found; if found they will not admit

paternity; if they do, they do not earn enough to pro- vide support. In sum, it is not possible to administer the program effectively. Therefore, it is obviously not cost-effective, since experience shows that it is not cost- effective.

4. The effort is nothing more than a reflection of racism, sexism, and hostility toward the poor.

It is worth examining this rationale in some detail. Is it soundly based on analytical studies, or is it simply an ideolog- ical assertion based on unproven assumptions? My reply to each point is presented below:

1. In response to the first point, child abuse has not been unknown in the history of mankind, though it is fair to say that only in the last decade have we come to a better understanding of the magnitude and depth of the problem. There is much that we do not know about the causes of child abuse, but what we do know from the records of cases brought to the courts is that it is generally committed by the parents or relatives in the home, not by the parent out of the home.

The notion that the children may be endangered if the ab- sent father is required to contribute to their support is not based on any study or analysis. Rather, it is an assertion based on a view of the low-income father, disproportionately black or His- panic, as unable to bear any responsibility without lashing out physically or emotionally at his children. Undoubtedly, there are such fathers, at all income levels and of all races, and moth- ers, too. But surely, and fortunately, experience and available data indicate that they constitute only a small fraction of the population.[4] And Congress has provided an exception to the requirement that the mother must cooperate in locating the fa- ther in cases in which it would not be in the best interest of the child.

Perhaps the argument would be made that even if one child were injured by a father unexpectedly infuriated by a court or- der for support, that would be one too many and must be avoided at all costs. If we were to insist on the universal ap- plication of this standard, we would not develop any new life-saving drugs or medical technologies; penicillin has saved thousands of lives, but it has killed a few and seriously threatened others who reacted badly to it. Nor could we build bridges or mine coal. Society cannot be organized to avoid all injury at all times to every individual and still achieve the important goals that substantially benefit the larger society. Some trade-offs are necessary; the goal can only be to reduce potential injury to the minimum.

It is essential to the effective administration of the child support program that the AFDC mother cooperate with the welfare administration by providing information to assist in the location of the father. Indeed, public assistance can be withheld if she does not cooperate. Issues of harassment or civil rights arise, or can arise, if the welfare worker believes the applicant is withholding information for any of a variety of reasons: she sees nothing in it for herself or the children since she will get her grant anyway, she may be getting some regular or irregular contributions from the father which she does not want to jeopardize, or she does not want any trouble or confrontation with the father.

But it is the worker's duty to probe for the information and not to accept at face value such statements as "I don't know where he lives," "I don't know where any of his family or friends live," or "I don't know what work he does or where he works." It must be borne in mind that very few out-of-wedlock children on welfare are the product of casual relationships. The vast majority of unmarried women on AFDC have had a relationship with the father for at least a year before becoming pregnant, and more than half for two or more years. Among the married women, fewer than 10 percent had been married for less than two years.[5] They must know something about the father. It is always possible that through prejudice, overzealousness, or even incompetence a worker may incorrectly assume lack of cooperation when, in fact, the mother does not have the necessary information and that an unreasonable denial of assistance will slip through the review process. But the denied applicant may apply for a fair hearing and, in the meantime, can obtain food stamps and emergency assistance if need can be shown.

Is it harassment or an abridgment of civil rights to insist on the mother's cooperation in naming and locating the father in exchange for obtaining public assistance? In Sweden, which has as liberal and extensive a social welfare program as any country and more than most, the mother applying for assistance is required to name the father and provide other relevant information so that he can be contacted and required to contribute to her support. If she does not cooperate, she is denied assistance. It is as simple and routine as that, and no one charges harrassment or denial of civil rights. The social welfare community in New York appears to insist that the client is always right and never says anything but the truth, the whole truth, and nothing but the truth. In the world we live in, this should not be regarded as the liberal view but as simple naivité.

2. In response to the second point, it has become fashionable in social welfare circles to accept any grouping of individuals who choose to consider themselves a "family" as such and in particular to regard the female-headed family as "normal" because of the enormous increase in the numbers of such families since the early 1960s. Since it is normal and therefore acceptable, financial support and other necessary services should be provided by the government. But we do not regard crime, drug abuse, or terrorism as normal or acceptable just because each has vastly increased in recent years, nor do we accept with equanimity rising absenteeism from schools and factories with its accompanying increase in school dropouts or declining productivity. To suggest that because the number of female-headed families has increased, government should be regarded as bearing the sole or even primary responsibility for support is circular and absurd reasoning. Of course, government must step in if there is no other source of support. But if the father is financially able to contribute, the mores of the general society require that he do so, and to ensure that he, in fact, does so, an effective enforcement system must be established.

3. In point 3 a series of "facts" has been assumed. Yet most of the social welfare community's "facts" with respect to the possibilities of finding fathers, establishing paternity, and obtaining support have proved ephemeral, and the assertion that

the program cannot become cost-effective has proved un-founded. In the country as a whole, as well as in many of the industrialized, urban states, including most of New York State, the program has been highly cost-effective. New York City has been the exception. (A fuller discussion of this issue is pre-sented later in this chapter.)

4. Where does this leave us with respect to the final and most emotional charge: that the child support program is racist, sexist, and anti-poor? It is true that in the country as a whole, blacks and Hispanics are disproportionately represented among AFDC clients and that, in many of the major cities, blacks and Hispanics constitute a substantial majority of the caseload. Per-force, they are the major target of the child support enforcement program. But the translation of this fact into racism must rest on the notion that one should not impose the same standards of family responsibility on black or Hispanic men as one would impose on white men in a comparable financial position. Why should we have lower expectations for blacks and Hispanics than for whites? Are they inferior? Are they naturally irresponsible? Don't they care at all about their children? Is it a characteristic of their race? If the responses to these questions are negative, as mine are, the charge of racism is nonsensical, as is the no-tion that efforts to obtain child support are sexist or anti-poor. Rather, the set of views expressed by the social welfare leaders becomes an elaborate justification, perhaps more aptly called a smoke screen, to permit an indiscriminate use of public assist-ance funds to redistribute income—not in accord with legisla-tive intent but in accord with the views of social justice held by many in the social welfare community.

As I have indicated, shortly after I became HRA commis-sioner in January 1978, I expressed my belief that the program could be made cost-effective in New York City. It was, how-ever, to prove much harder than I had imagined; a major diffi-culty lay in the attitudes of the judges in the Family Court. This topic brings me to the role of the courts in the administration of the IV-D program and to an important illustration of how the courts can in effect contravene legislative policy through judicial intervention into the administration of a program.

The Attitudes of the Family Courts

The Family Court has an essential role in the implementation of the child support program. Only the court can make the legal determination of paternity, the basis for requiring support payments; only the court can issue an enforceable support order; and only the court can enforce it. Even support agreements entered into voluntarily cannot be enforced unless they have been submitted to the court and a confirmatory order issued.

It must be recognized that the IV-D program, designed as it was to promote a vastly increased and aggressive effort to locate absent fathers and obtain support, placed a heavy additional burden on the Family Court, already overburdened with a growing volume of juvenile delinquency and child abuse cases, issues of much public concern requiring prompt attention. Further, although the federal government reimburses 75 percent of state and local costs entailed in the operation of the IV-D program, it was not until 1980 that such costs were defined to include court costs (but not judges' salaries), and even then only costs in excess of the 1978 level became reimbursable. The fiscal crisis in the city precluded any increase in Family Court staff financed from city funds; indeed, it imposed a decrease.

In any event, a host of administrative problems arose in relation to processing child support cases through the Family Courts, and a large volume of recriminatory correspondence was exchanged between state and city officials, on the one hand, and Joseph B. Williams, administrative judge of the Family Court in New York City, on the other.*

---

*It began as early as April 1975, before the new program was actually under way, when state and city officials shared their concern that Judge Williams had directed Family Court judges to dismiss any support case in which the client did not appear at a scheduled hearing, instead of rescheduling it for a later date. The result was that the respondent's support payments and any arrearages that may have been due were canceled. Mutual recrimination reached a crescendo in 1978 and 1979 on matters ranging from obtaining permission to visit the courts to the number of IV-D cases that would be accepted by courts for processing each month and the growing backlog of unheard cases.

But while the Family Court had legitimate problems in terms of limited staff and additional work loads, one must look to the attitudes of the judges toward the program to understand why it has been so much less effective in New York City than in cities such as Detroit, which has a caseload similar in size and characteristics to New York. The Community Council's 1977 study, already quoted, reported that "many judges expressed very negative feelings toward IV-D . . . they said it had been imposed on them: some felt that it diminished their function by making the courts act as a collection agency for IV-D." Judge Williams took a strong position against the view of the Family Court as a collection agency. In a letter of September 28, 1977, responding to the director of the Office of Management and Budget (OMB), he wrote, "The need for the city to achieve revenue collection goals and your opinion that the Family Court should enforce executive agency policy regarding ability to pay and arrearages—your position ignores the essential nature of the proceeding. The decisions rendered in these, as in all other matters before the Court, are and must continue to be, based on the statutory requirements of the relevant legislation and remain within the sphere of judicial discretion and outside the pressures of executive branch expediency. The Court cannot view itself as a revenue collection agency when rendering IV-D decisions."

What was really at issue was not whether the Family Court should be a "collection agency" for the executive branch—that was not the view of state or city officials—but whether the court and the judges were going to abide by the spirit as well as the letter of the legislation and the executive regulations, or whether they were going to exploit judicial discretion without limit. That the latter was probable became evident to me in July 1978 when I visited the Brooklyn Family Court, where I had a long talk with Judge Philip D. Roache and sat in his court to listen to three cases of child support. Shortly thereafter, I wrote Mayor Koch describing what I heard and saw, and I will quote extensively from the memorandum.

I wrote the mayor:

Judge Roache indicated a lack of sympathy with the IV-D program and I shall try to give the flavor of a series of complaints he made as follows [Judge Roache's comments are in italics; mine are not]:

1. *What is the point of bringing in all these 18 or 19 year olds who have not seen their fathers for 15 years to try to establish paternity? It's an utter waste of time.* I then responded with the fact that there are very, very few such cases. The great bulk of cases dealt with are young children.

2. *What was the use of bringing the fathers into court since they are all on public assistance?* I said, on the basis of available figures, this clearly was not true. Most of the fathers were not on public assistance. Further, even when they were, we might want to establish paternity in case they later become self-supporting. But we did *not* try to obtain support while they were on public assistance.

3. *What is the use of bringing these men in for support since none of them are earning very much?* I said some were not earning much and others were earning enough to provide some support according to the state standard which allowed the "absent father" to retain enough income to maintain the Bureau of Labor Statistics lower level standard of independent living. Judge Roache rejected the state standard and said, he "knew better what a man could afford to contribute to the support of his child" . . . .

I then moved into Court with Judge Roache and observed the procedure in three child support/paternity cases. Among the six people involved, all were young—somewhere in their twenties. None were married. The three children involved were all very young. The three men were working and all three readily admitted paternity. With respect to this latter point, I felt that Judge Roache in his efforts to inform the men of their right to deny paternity overstressed the burdens this could impose on them without any counterbalancing statement indicating that if they were the fathers of the children, they had a responsibility toward them.

More disturbing, was what could almost be called a farce in terms of determining what the father could afford to pay toward support. Judge Roache asked what they paid for rent, a question each was generally able to answer; whether accurately or not, one could not say. He then asked how much they spent on food and what other bills they had—questions which each of the three men found utterly confusing;

clearly they had no idea. The three men respectively earned
$91, $120 and $140 per week, net of taxes. In one case, the
man offered to pay $15 per week, but Judge Roache decided
that he should pay only $10; this was the man earning $120
a week who was living with his aunt and paying $25 a week
for rent and board. The man earning $140 was already mak-
ing a support contribution and the amount was not di-
vulged or reviewed by the court.

I was later advised by staff who are frequently in Judge
Roache's court that even the above sums, which are substantially below the state standard, were higher than he ordinarily allows and may have been due to my presence in
court.

After receiving the above memorandum the mayor wrote
David Ross, Administrative Judge for Courts in New York City,
on July 25, 1978, bringing the problem to his attention and requesting some corrective action. In conclusion he said, "What
is particularly painful to me is to learn that last year the City of
New York collected under this program approximately $15 mil-
lion while Detroit in a similar period of time, collected approximately $50 million. It would appear to me that the missing in-
gredient is the will of the Family Court judges to assist by
carrying out their responsibilities."

Certainly the willingness, or unwillingness, of the judges
to fulfill their responsibilities in the child support program is a
major factor influencing the effectiveness of the program. The
Community Council study which, as indicated above, is not
generally supportive of the IV-D program, nevertheless states
that "one of the major factors contributing to the success of the
Michigan program is the attitude of the judiciary. Support enforcement is considered a priority issue throughout the state.
Moreover, there seems to be wide public awareness that support enforcement measures will be utilized by the court and this
in itself serves as a deterrent to noncompliance."

I have quoted my memorandum of my discussion with
Judge Roache at length because his attitudes and views, though
not held by all Family Court judges, are typical of so many that
they exercise a controlling influence on the outcome of the

IV-D program in the city and state. There are, in my view, three major strands to an explanation of why the judges behave as they do with respect to the child support obligation.

First, to the extent that the law permits, judges jealously guard the prerogative of judicial discretion. While Family Court judges are aware of the extraordinary variation in the value of the support orders issued in seemingly similar circumstances, they defend the practice in discussions with state and city officials on the grounds that only the judge can make a correct appraisal of the individual circumstances in each case. In brief, each judge tends to regard himself in the image of Solomon. Limits to his discretion are considered not only as diminishing his power and authority but as demeaning to his status.

Second, the politics of judicial appointment in both city and state, where a liberal, humanitarian tradition has generally prevailed under both Democratic and Republican administrations, has meant that, by and large, persons of liberal persuasion have been appointed to the Family Courts as well as to other courts. Exception can hardly be taken to that. The difficulty lies in the way the liberal tradition has been interpreted in the public assistance and child support programs. We see again the over-reaction to past and present discrimination against minorities, against blacks in particular, materializing in an uncritical acceptance of what are supposed to be facts but are not, in lower expectations with regard to parental responsibility among low-income families, and in a general sense that a little extra income redistribution, over and above legislative intent, is not such a bad idea in an insufficiently just society. So, why engage in a strict administration of the child support program instead of relying more heavily than necessary on public assistance?

Third, one cannot ignore the politics involved in the appointment of blacks and Hispanics to the judiciary. This is not to say that adequate representation of minorities in the judiciary is not an essential element of a just society; indeed, such representation was long overdue. Rather, it is to say that, by and large, those who have the necessary political clout along

with the substantive credentials to obtain the appointments—
and the reappointments—are likely to carry with them the whole
ideological baggage of the activist minority community. This
ideology stresses discrimination and poverty and the obligation
of the white community to redress grievances to the virtual exclusion of recognition of the advances made in education, jobs,
and income or the obligations which rest on the members
of any community to fulfill their responsibilities to the extent
possible.

Mayor Koch, who has not been exactly restrained in his
public criticism of judges in the criminal as well as the Family
Court, reappointed Judge Roache when his term expired in 1980.
Such was the political reality. I must add that what I have said
with respect to the appointment of black and Hispanic judges
applies in substantial measure to white judges as well; many of
them carry the same ideological baggage. But there is more diversity of views among the white political leadership and among
white judges.

It is worth pointing out that while the unemployment rate
of 14.0 percent as of November 1981 among black adult males
was more than twice the rate among white adult males, 86.0
percent of black adult males in the labor force were employed.[6]
Of course, some percentage of black males aged fifteen to sixty-
five have dropped out of the labor force or are in the under-
ground labor market and more difficult to reach. But not every
black absent father is unemployed, or, if he is working, earning
only a minimum wage.

Neither my memorandum nor the mayor's letter to Judge
Ross had much effect. The attitude and actions of many of the
Family Court judges continued to be hostile toward the program, as reflected in their responses to the two major matters
which control the outcome of the effort to achieve child support
from absent parents. These are the amount of support payments
and the methods used to enforce the support obligation ordered
by the court. It was through its resistance to the administrative
tools provided in state legislation or NYSDSS administrative di-

rectives that the court impeded the implementation of the policy enacted in the child support program.

How Much Should the Father Pay?

Brief reference was made in the opening pages of this chapter to the omission from laws governing divorce and the father's obligation to support of any but the most general directive to the court to determine a level of support which is "just and proper." Appellate Court decisions also provide trial judges with little guidance.[7] Many laws governing punishment for criminal activity are similar in their vagueness about the penalty which should be prescribed for a particular crime. And, as in the case of criminal penalties, court orders for support present a bewildering variety of decisions in similar situations.

Federal law and regulations establishing the IV-D program did not require the use of a formula to determine the amount of a child support obligation in either AFDC or non-AFDC cases (except in states where the obligation is established by some process other than a court order, such as an administrative hearing system). In some states or localities, however, some efforts have been made to establish uniform guidelines. In Michigan, for example, local judges "have devised a system that has produced some measure of regularity and rough equity, even though it fails to reflect a coherent set of principles."[8] Schedules developed at the county level, generally adhered to within the county, relate the amount of the support order to the number of children in the family and the earnings after taxes of the non-custodial parent. At the request of Seattle judges, a schedule was also developed for use in that city which is similar to the Michigan counties' standards.

In 1975, while announcing that the Family Court retained full discretion to order the amount of support in a particular case, New York State established a formula for the guidance of county welfare agency staff members and required them to use the formula to determine the minimum amount of support to be requested in petitioning the Family Court. It was based on reserving for the absent parent an amount equal to a subsistence level of living and taking the remainder for the AFDC family. It was widely, if not universally, ignored by the Family Courts throughout the state.

Some months after I became Deputy Commissioner for Income Maintenance at the New York State Department of Social Services in August 1975, I came to the view that the existing formula was so draconian as to invite rejection by the courts. A more realistic formula was needed, and the department proceeded to develop one. The new formula permitted the absent father and his family, if he had one, to retain sufficient income to maintain the BLS lower-level living standard. In September 1975, the gross income required to maintain this standard for a family of four was $8,189; in September 1980 prices, it was $14,393. The comparable figures for the one-person family were $3,275 and $5,700 (many absent fathers have not remarried and are therefore one-person families).* Further, in order not to destroy incentives, the formula provided that only a portion of the excess above the BLS standard would be required for support payments, a proportion starting at 25 percent at the lower income levels and gradually increasing to a maximum of 65 percent when "excess" income equaled $300 a month or more. In addition to income, provision was made for equal sharing of liquid assets between the absent father and the AFDC family, based on the total number of persons in both families. One new note we introduced was to require that the earnings of the absent father's new wife or live-in girlfriend be included in the calculation of his income for purposes of determining the excess available for support of the AFDC family. Nevertheless, the formula was much more generous to the absent parent and his

---

*A gross income of $6,097 is achieved by someone working thirty-five hours a week at the minimum wage; at $6.60 an hour, the average hourly earnings in November 1980 of nonsupervisory production workers in manufacturing industries in the city, annual income would equal $12,012.

new family than the earlier one. We anticipated that though it was not mandatory, it would be widely accepted by the Family Court judges. We were to be disappointed.

In early 1976, counsel to NYSDSS discussed the desirability of a uniform system for establishing support obligations before the Family Court Judges Association in New York City. He reported that the judges were divided on the issue. Some felt that some uniformity, possibly in the shape of uniform factors to be considered, might be desirable. Others, probably the majority, were not even receptive to this approach. They adamantly opposed any system that threatened to interfere with their absolute discretion. Despite the lack of enthusiasm expressed by the Family Court judges, the new formula, with some minor modifications, was issued in May 1976.

What happened then? First, the support formula came under attack from the social welfare community, as reflected in the Community Council's *Who Should Support the Children?* It recommended eliminating the use of the formula in New York City: "We cannot speak for its continued utilization in the rest of the state. For New York City, however, the formula is unrealistic. It sets too high a level of support for the absent parent." Its justification for the last statement was that voluntary agreements rarely reach the formula level and that Family Court judges "generally ignore" the formula. But that was why the formula was introduced—to raise the level of payments which derived either from voluntary agreement or from judges' decisions not based on reasoned criteria.

As was not infrequent in the council's report, there is a discrepancy between its recommendation and its fact finding. In its observations on the courts, the report stated, "There appeared to be no consistency either among judges or even from the same judge as to the amount of support ordered, even in cases which on the surface appeared similar, e.g., the respondents had the same net weekly earnings." It also reported that the judges thought the requirements for support were too high and were antagonistic because they regarded the formula as an infringement on their discretion. And, finally, it stated: "It was hard to determine how judges actually made their decisions on the amount of the support order."*

It must also be said that many HRA staff members involved in the child support program—coming as they did out of the social work profession or, if from other professions, steeped in the notion that the absent fathers were unemployed, poor, or otherwise overburdened—were also unsympathetic to the formula and were less than aggressive in trying to obtain voluntary agreements more closely related to the formula. In any event, data prepared by HRA's Bureau of Child Support on the basis of court orders issued in October 1977 indicated that court-ordered support payments averaged only 54.3 percent of the state standard. This was true despite the fact that a 1977 amendment to the Family Court Act provided that the support formula should be given the weight of *prima facie* evidence of ability to support at the formula level.

Early in 1978, after I became HRA commissioner, we began to work with NYSDSS to obtain legislation mandating the use of the state formula by the Family Court judges. At this time,

---

*Even more curious, the Council, while objecting to the state formula for support payments, recommended that the administrative judge should issue some guidelines for the judges and suggested the Council's *Guide to Determine the Ability of an Absent Parent to Provide Support* as a model. This guide, like the state's formula, allows the absent father to retain sufficient income to maintain the BLS lower-level standard for himself and his new family, but it recommends that a constant 90 percent of the excess be claimed for support payments, a far higher level than claimed in the state formula, which graduated from 25 percent at the lower level to a maximum of 65 percent at higher income levels. The guide was prepared with financial support from the Office of Child Support and the Social and Rehabilitation Service, U.S. Department of Health, Education and Welfare, and with the help of an advisory committee consisting of experts in home economics, officials concerned with the child support program, and social workers. Because of the source of its financing and the nature of the advisory committee, the study was not submitted to the Community Council's board of directors for approval. It is possible that neither the board nor the committee which prepared *Who Should Support the Children?* understood the implications of the guide.

city and state appeared to be in complete agreement on the importance of obtaining adherence to the formula in the Family Courts. The March 1978 report to the governor and legislature on the program stated: "The Department will intensify its efforts to increase acceptance by Family Court judges of the Department's support formula as a reasonable measure of capacity to pay child support." The report went on, however, to indicate that the department was engaged in discussions with representatives of the Family Court Judges Association "aimed at securing agreement on a formula they could support." And in its January 1979 report to the governor and legislature, the department listed first among the judiciary's requirements for a workable formula "acknowledgment of judicial latitude in fixing the amount of support."

State officials in a memorandum distributed to all local agencies described the conceptual basis of the proposed new formula as "a range of monies based on the absent parent's net worth which provides for the support of dependent children while permitting the absent parent to retain $80 to $140 a week net of income and social security taxes, health insurance, union dues and a few other items to maintain his household."* Why $80 to $140 is not clear, and what relationship these figures have to size of family is at best obscure. (A net income of $140 a week would not permit maintenance of the BLS lower level of living for a four-person family at 1978 prices, though $80 would be above the standard for a single person.) Further, a wide range is permitted with respect to the proportion of the excess to be taken for child support—from 35 to 75 percent if the excess is less than $100 per week, up to 70 to 80 percent if it is over $225

---

*In early August, we had advised state officials that analysis of six actual cases revealed that at the lower end of the range, the new formula falls far below the support levels provided in the 1976 formula and is only a few dollars more at the higher level. We added, "The courts in applying the variables . . . are more likely to lean toward the lower end. This could only result in lower support orders than we are currently receiving."

per week. Finally, while the judges "must take account" of the formula, they are not bound by it.

I wrote the state commissioner on August 30, 1978, that "in my view, if this proposed formula were adopted, it would cripple New York City's opportunity to achieve an equitable formula to press on the Family Court. The latitude given the judges in the proposed order is equivalent to the new support orders they are currently issuing. It appears that the formula was constructed to satisfy the Family Court rather than claim an appropriate amount that we should be seeking."

Despite the city's protests, the new state formula was issued in October 1978. State officials had hoped that if they bowed to judicial discretion, higher collections would be obtained in the city. It was not to be. In December 1978, before the new formula was implemented, the average court order for support payments equaled $31.31 per week in cases where the issue of paternity did not arise; it dropped to $30.28 in December 1979. In cases involving out-of-wedlock children where paternity had to be established, the average court order rose slightly from $18.17 per week to $19.33.[9] In the first type of case, average support orders reached no more than two-thirds of the median established in the formula; and in the second, which constitutes 50 percent of all court-ordered support payments, support orders averaged only 55 percent of the median. In other words, the Family Court judges were setting the support payments at the lower end of the formula range, as could have been anticipated.

The state legislature has not intervened in the matter of the level of support payments since 1978; apparently it is unready to grasp this particular nettle. Judicial discretion reigns supreme. As it is exercised in many areas in the country, but particularly in New York City, it reflects a reluctance to impose any significant burden on the absent father to support his children and demonstrates little interest in reducing the burden on the public treasury represented by the AFDC program.* We shall

---

*Comprehensive data are not available, but information presented to state officials by some of the welfare administrators in upstate New York

see further reflections of the "ideology of the disadvantaged" in the courts' actions with respect to state legislative efforts to improve the location of fathers and the enforcement of support orders.

Enforcing the Support Obligation

Establishing the level of support is one important step in the process of providing for children in both AFDC and non-AFDC families, but it is not the only one. The next step is to enforce the order, and this, too, has proved a formidable problem. The NYSDSS annual report on the child support program, issued in March 1978, stated: "The failure to secure compliance with support obligations once they have been established by either voluntary agreements or court order is perhaps the single most serious weakness currently plaguing the state's IV-D program. Not surprisingly, the problem is most severe in New York City. In the third quarter of 1977, collections were received for only 37 percent of the cases in which an obligation had been established. The total arrearages reported for current IV-D cases in New York City is extremely high—and it is growing month by month." The same report indicated that between August 1977 and January 1978, arrearages increased from $20.2 million to $28.3 million; the proportion of cases in arrears remained steady at about 40 percent.

Indeed, it was not surprising that collections were in bad shape in New York City, since the Family Courts had rather consistently opposed and resisted legislative efforts to strengthen enforcement procedures. Each year beginning in 1976, the legislature passed some amendments to the laws governing the child support program, amendments designed to improve the ef-

counties indicates that Family Court judges tend to order more generous payments to non-AFDC than to AFDC families from fathers in the same financial circumstances. The theory is the AFDC family will get the same amount of money from the state anyway, so why bother the father to make support payments.

fectiveness of the operation or, more particularly, to improve the potential for effective enforcement. The three most important provided for mail service of the summons to the absent father for appearance in court, permitted the establishment of hearing examiners to elicit information about the father's ability to provide support, and authorized the issuance of automatic payroll deduction orders to become effective in the event of nonpayment of the court support orders.

One of the major problems faced in pursuing the child support program, and one that was excessively time-consuming, was locating the father in the sense of finding out where he lived or worked, and then making actual contact with him to obtain information about his financial status and to serve the summons for the court appearance. The AFDC mother is required to cooperate in the first part of this endeavor, but often she does not know, or claims not to know, where the father lives or works. The Bureau of Child Support is then left with the onerous task of trying to determine his whereabouts with the aid of the federal and state parent locator services or, since 1977, when it was permitted by law, with the aid of private investigators. But even when the father's whereabouts are discovered, it may be difficult to find him at home to serve the summons.

In order to save staff time and to ensure delivery of a summons before the father moved again, HRA began in 1977 to mail the summons in cases where the father had not responded to a letter requesting him to appear at the Bureau of Child Support for an interview. It was within the Family Court's discretion to accept delivery of a summons by mail, but most of the judges refused to do so and, therefore, refused to issue an order requiring the father's presence in court. The issue was not resolved until an amendment was adopted at the 1978 legislative session, removing the issue from the court's general discretion and permitting mail service in all support cases. But more than a year had been lost in fruitless negotiation.

The pattern was similar with respect to the issue of hearing examiners. As has been indicated, Family Court judges had been complaining vociferously about the heavy burden the IV-D program placed on the courts; indeed, they had a justifiable complaint. Further, a two- to three-month delay was common between locating the father, filing the petition, and scheduling the court hearing. This gap meant lost time in beginning to collect support payments and frequently led to the nonappearance of the father in court—a serious matter, since the court would rarely issue an order if the father was not present. The legislature tried to meet the problem in 1977 by permitting the Family Court to use hearing examiners in support proceedings. While the Family Court judges would have to issue the paternity determination and the order for support, the preliminary work done by the hearing examiner would save the judge's time.

Did the Family Court in the city rush to take advantage of the new legislation? Not exactly. In response to a letter from the director of the Office of Management and Budget, Judge Williams wrote in late September 1977 that the enabling legislation had only become effective on September 1, 1977, and that the Appellate Division was still working on the rules for the conduct of proceedings by hearing examiners. A month later the rules had not yet been issued. Commissioner J. Henry Smith wrote to the presiding justices at the Appellate Division in the First and Second Departments, urging immediate action and indicating that he "had hoped the Hearing Examiner system would be in place by September 1, the effective date of the legislation. We have learned to our great disappointment, that you have not yet made the determination necessary to effectuate the legislation in your Department." The courts, of course, had had some months between the passage of the legislation and its effective date to prepare the rules, but several more months were to elapse before they were issued.

By the spring of 1978, the court was preparing to screen candidates for the hearing examiner panels. On this occasion, Irwin Brooks, Assistant Commissioner for Income Support, wrote to Judge Williams to express HRA's "hope that in reviewing the qualifications of attorneys to act as Hearing Examiners, you will weigh their attitudes on the obligations of parents to support their children." He added that "public assistance should not be

viewed as a substitute source of support by a parent who refuses to meet his moral and legal obligations to his family. As
provided by statute, the parent should be compelled to support
his family in accordance with his means . . . I hope that the
Screening Committee will keep this in mind and choose attorneys who will abide by the spirit of Title 4 of the Family Court
Act." As commissioner, I also wrote Judge Williams to say that
I particularly wanted to inscribe my vote for Brooks's suggestion
that qualifications of hearing examiners should include "a general adherence to the notion of parental responsibility for the
support of their children to the extent that they are able to do
so." We received no written response from Judge Williams to
these letters, and whether our suggestion was taken into account, we do not know. It is a sad commentary on the situation
that we felt it necessary to write as we did.

In any event, the legislature became annoyed with the slow
progress of the courts in responding to the grant of permission
to establish panels of hearing examiners. As a result, in its 1978
session, a new amendment was passed requiring the establishment of panels of hearing examiners and the promulgation of
rules for the referral of support procedures to such examiners.
Eventually, a hearing panel was established in each of the bor-
oughs. But, once again, time and potential support payments
were lost.

As must be evident from this description of the process
required to obtain a child support order, the effort involved is
enormous. The effort is all for naught, however, if the order is
not enforced. In the third quarter of 1977, as indicated above,
payments were not obtained on almost two-thirds of the court
orders issued. The most effective tool for ensuring payments—
and one that is far less harsh than jailing, which is also an effective tool—is arranging for payroll deductions and for direct
payment of the sum deducted by the employer to the Bureau of
Child Support.

Unless an automatic payroll deduction order is obtained at
the same time the child support order is issued, it is necessary
for Bureau of Child Support staff to go back to the court, a pro-

cess which consumes not only staff time but also time in which arrearages build up and repayment becomes more difficult. This payroll deduction system has been used with considerable success in Michigan and Massachusetts. Family Court judges in New York, however, were extremely reluctant to issue payroll deduction orders.* The reason given frequently by the judges was their concern over the possibility of dismissal by the employer because of the bookkeeping nuisance it entailed, though there was little evidence that this, in fact, happened.

The legislature responded to this problem, as it had to others in the 1978 legislation, by requiring that support orders issued after January 1, 1979, provide for an automatic payroll deduction order in the event that the respondent failed to keep up with his payments. And in 1979 the state made it illegal for an employer to dismiss an employee because of the imposition of such an order. Only a month after the 1978 law became effective I found it necessary to inform the mayor in a memorandum that "after four weeks of observation, I am distressed to advise you that most of the Family Court judges have decided not to issue this order stating on the record that the law is unconstitutional." HRA had again to return to the court to request a payroll deduction order in the event of nonpayment. In enacting this legislation, the legislature aimed to avoid this added paperwork and lost time and to relieve the already crowded court calendar.

HRA instituted an appeal in a case in which a man was earning $154 per week and was ordered to pay $15 for the support of his wife and four children; the court refused to issue the automatic payroll deduction order because of the possibility that the man, who worked in a small nursing home, might be dismissed. Approximately one year later, the Appellate Division in the First Department issued a unanimous decision upholding the constitutionality of the statute and reversing the Family Court

---

*According to the 1977 Community Council report, only seven payroll deduction orders were issued out of 398 cases observed, despite large arrears and a repetitive history of nonpayment in many cases.

decision, which had held that the automatic requirement violated the employee's right to due process and equal protection. But that decision solved our problem only in the First Department—Manhattan and the Bronx. Family Court judges in the Second Department—Brooklyn and Queens—refused to recognize the authority of the Appellate Court in the First Department. Not until HRA brought another case, and won in the Second Department as well, would all the Family Court judges permit an automatic payroll deduction order. Thus, full implementation did not begin until August 1980, twenty months after the law was supposed to have become effective.

One further legislative effort was made in 1978 to restrict the court's discretion in child support matters. The court was prohibited from reducing or canceling arrears unless good cause was shown and a written record of the basis for a decision to decrease or cancel was made. This amendment was designed to prevent a common Catch-22 situation: payroll deduction orders were not issued, mail service of summons was not accepted, time passed, arrears piled up, and the court canceled the arrears.

WHAT HAPPENED TO SUPPORT COLLECTIONS?

One may ask whether it made much difference what the leaders of the social welfare community in New York thought and said and what the Family Court judges generally thought and did. Has the record of collections of support payments in the city over the five-year period since Title IV-D came into effect in August 1975 been any worse than the record in the rest of the country? The answer is yes, it did make a difference, and yes, the city's record is worse—much worse.

The federal Office of Child Support Enforcement from time to time issues its best-dressed list—those states with the highest rates of collections in relation to total expenditures for the AFDC program. New York State has never made the list, mainly because of New York City. In the country as a whole, collections on behalf of AFDC families more than doubled between 1976 and 1978, increasing from $203.6 million to $471.6 million. A further increase of 16.1 percent occurred between 1978 and 1979 and an additional 10 percent rise was achieved in 1980, when total collections reached $602.3 million. During the same five-year period, collections on behalf of non-AFDC families almost tripled, rising from $308.1 million to $871 million. Collections on behalf of AFDC and non-AFDC families exceeded expenditures by more than three to one. In New York City, collections during the same five-year period increased only about 4 to 5 percent per year and still do not exceed total expenditures. Because of the formula for distributing collections among the three levels of government, however, the New York City treasury still benefits.

It can be unfair to compare New York State, and certainly New York City, with the country as a whole. The more appropriate comparison is with the other highly urbanized, industrial states. In this case, New York fares even worse. IV-D cases with collections as a percentage of total IV-D caseloads for these states in fiscal 1980 are shown below: [10]

TOTAL (all states reporting)	*10.8*
Massachusetts	42.6
Connecticut	32.0
Michigan	22.8
Pennsylvania	15.6
New Jersey	12.4
California	9.5
Ohio	8.8
Illinois	7.8
New York	7.8

New York State collects in only about a sixth as many cases, proportionately, as does Massachusetts, a quarter as many as Connecticut, and a third as many as Michigan. The New York City ratio is at the appallingly low level of 3.7 percent of cases.

In terms of collections as a proportion of total AFDC payments, the figures for fiscal 1980 are as follows:[11]

TOTAL (all states reporting)	5.2
Michigan	8.0
Connecticut	7.0
Massachusetts	6.3
New Jersey	6.1
Ohio	4.8
California	4.6
Pennsylvania	4.6
New York	3.4
Illinois	1.6

Again, except for Illinois, New York State is the lowest, and
New York City is lower still, with collections of less than 2
percent. Michigan, though lower than Massachusetts and Connecticut in terms of the proportion of AFDC cases for which
collections are obtained, exceeds these states in the proportion
of AFDC expenditures recouped through support payments. It
has been able to accomplish this even though it has one of the
higher welfare standards in the country and was in a deep
recession in 1980 (as it still is) because of the precipitous decline
in automobile production; its unemployment rate is about 16
percent.

Massachusetts and Michigan again lead in terms of the number of dollars of AFDC child support collected for every dollar
of AFDC expenditures for the IV-D program. New York State is
at the bottom of the list. New York's figure is so low because of
New York City, which collected only 54 cents per dollar of expenditures. The following tabulation shows collections for every
dollar of AFDC IV-D program expenditures in fiscal 1980: [12]

TOTAL (all states reporting)	$1.56
Massachusetts	3.80
Michigan	3.54
Connecticut	2.29

Pennsylvania	1.92
Ohio	1.67
California	1.38
New Jersey	1.36
Illinois	1.10
New York	0.98

On any index one may choose to compare New York City with other urban areas, the city's record is dismal. Its only competitor for low man on the totem pole is Illinois, influenced mainly by Chicago. Are there lessons to be learned from other states? Are we bereft of means to improve the effectiveness of the program in the city and to bring it in line with the achievements in Detroit or Boston, or at least in Philadelphia?

WHAT CAN BE DONE?

Michigan is frequently cited for its superior achievement in the child support program. Several factors explain its success. First, it began its program earlier than most other states, which did little in response to the 1967 federal legislation; Michigan, however, took it seriously. Second, it developed its enforcement system through the prosecuting attorneys and, in particular, developed the "friend of the court" system, which has proven extremely effective. A friend of the court, who is appointed for life, has a variety of duties; he makes home visits to determine suitability in regard to custody, verifies earnings, recommends to the courts the amount of support which should be granted, enforces support obligations, and recommends modifications in support orders when they appear out of line with economic circumstances. The Michigan Department of Social Services works closely with the prosecuting attorneys and the friend of the court and provides some financial support for them. Third, the judiciary is persuaded of the validity of the notion that parents are responsible for the support of children and is vigorous in its determination to enforce the child support program. Fourth, the program has the support of the unions—more particularly, of *the* union in Michigan, the United Auto Workers. Major auto manufacturers and the unions cooperate with the program to ensure enforcement, and wide use is made of the payroll deduction order.

John Dempsey, Commissioner of Social Services in Michigan, in summarizing the results of the Michigan child support program in the spring of 1978 noted not only improved services to clients, a reduction in welfare abuse, and restoration of public confidence in the welfare system, but also an apparent trend toward reconciliation between spouses, making the family intact again. That finding means, in all probability, that the family can be removed from the welfare rolls completely.

The Michigan program cannot simply be copied in New York City. For one thing, no one in his or her right mind would suggest looking to the district attorneys' offices in the city for vigorous prosecution of absent fathers in child support cases. They are too overburdened with other problems. For another, it is unlikely that the Family Court judges, with their present attitudes, would pay any more attention to the recommendations made by a friend of the court for support payments than they do to the Department of Social Services.

But the Michigan experience makes it clear that unless a change in the attitudes of a large majority of the Family Court judges can be achieved, we cannot expect much improvement in the effectiveness of the child support program. Basically, progress can be made only through the political process, and in New York City that means, in the first instance, the mayor. As indicated earlier, Mayor Koch has not been sparing in his criticism of decisions of Family Court judges in child support cases, but he has not always followed through when it came to appointments and reappointments. He needs to do so and to trust the public which elected him not to withdraw its support if he refuses to reappoint judges who do not support the notion that fathers have an obligation to support their children.

The Michigan experience also suggests that a strong effort should be made by the governor's and mayor's offices, as well as by state and local social services officials, to enlist the aid of the unions in promoting the child support program among their members. New York is not like Detroit, where one union predominates. But five or six, especially if they included District Council 37, the municipal workers' union, would cover a substantial segment of the city's union membership. The unions could be influential with their own members who should be making support payments, and they could help create a general climate in which it is taken as a given that parents have an obligation to support their children.

Federal officials involved with the child support program are also concerned about the low level of court-ordered support payments; they have recently inaugurated an effort through the Judicial College to raise judicial understanding of the problem. The size of the effort is such, however, that even if it is successful, it will take many years to permeate through the nation's Family Courts. The more expeditious method would be for Congress to require each state to develop an appropriate formula for use in its courts and for the states to require judges to use the state formula in determining the support payment. In sum, judicial discretion needs to be very substantially narrowed with respect to the amount of support, as it has been with respect to other matters.

New York State has now mandated a variety of procedures to facilitate the court process: mail service of the summons, establishment of hearing examiner panels, and improved enforcement through automatic payroll deductions, limitation on the cancellation of arrearages, and a variety of other detailed procedures. But those involved in implementing the program must still have the will to make it work if it is to work well; and that requires informed and vigorous public support for the effort. It is a subject which the city's major newspapers should cover at least as intensively as they cover the public assistance and food stamp programs, and yet they rarely do so.

The leaders of the social welfare community have been successful in creating a climate of opinion unfavorable to the child support program among those who have a significant role to play in its implementation—that is, the judiciary and the large body of workers in HRA who do the daily work of interviewing clients and absent fathers and handling the details of the cases as they go through the court process. They should not be left unchallenged. The problem has not been high on the agenda of other civic groups in the city. It is time that they took it up. It is an issue which ought to be of concern to the major women's groups. They have favored the child support program on the national level but do not appear to have devoted their attention to the implementation of the programs at the state or local level. It could be useful if they took up the cudgels for an effective program in New York as well as in other major cities. The stakes are high—not only in potential savings of public funds but, more important, in the program's potential as a deterrent to family break-up and the deleterious consequences for the children involved.

CHAPTER 4

Why Did We Mess Up the Food Stamp Program for So Long?

The Food Stamp program, established in its present form in 1964, grew slowly at first, mainly replacing the distribution of food commodities. But as surveys undertaken in the late 1960s began to uncover serious malnutrition in the country, particularly in the South, Congress responded with a series of legislative changes to ameliorate the problem. The program quickly expanded—reflecting in part the completion of the process of replacing the distribution of commodities, but mainly reflecting the substantial increase in benefit levels enacted in the 1971 amendments to the original Food Stamp Act.

With the 1971 modifications, the program became the first federal program with national eligibility standards based on need. Further, unlike AFDC, it was available to all types of families, not just those headed by women or disabled men. To achieve an adequate diet for all Americans, food stamps were available to the working poor, as well as to those on welfare. Participation, which had reached 9.4 million recipients in 1971, rose to 12.7 million in 1974 and then jumped to 17.1 million in 1975, as unemployment rose during the 1974–1975 recession. The number of recipients continued to rise through 1978, dropped in 1979, and reached a new high of 22 million in 1980, another recession year.

An adequate diet for all became—and must remain—a high-priority goal. A broad consensus supports this goal; yet by 1975 the size of the program and the effectiveness of its administration were open to question. A Congressional Research Service Issue Brief on *Food Stamp Program Reform* opened with the words: "In 1975 and 1976, the expansion of the Food Stamp Program and the consequent increased visibility of what critics saw as abuses, flaws, and inequities in the program, focused national attention on the need for changes in the food stamp policies. Concern was expressed about the cost of the program, the degree to which eligibility was overextended, the program's administrative effectiveness and complexity, the accessibility of the program to eligible households, and the degree of inequity in the benefit distribution."[1] The program remained controversial and became one of the Reagan administration's targets for a substantial budget cut.

To understand why the program came under indictment and the course of developments during the last five years, one must examine the nature of the conflict and the lineup of forces on the various issues. Briefly, the conflict involves the balance to be struck between ensuring access to the program and ensuring its integrity. The battle cry shouted by all was "adequate nutrition for all Americans." The battleground was the nitty-gritty of rules and regulations governing the administration of the program, in particular the methods for determining and checking eligibility. The conflict is common to many "income tested" programs—that is, programs in which eligibility is determined by family income and available assets in relation to the size of the family and allowable deductions or disregards of gross income. It was, of course, evident in the AFDC program. Many similarities can indeed be pointed at between policy and administrative developments in the AFDC and the Food Stamp programs, but the cast of characters is different. Moreover, the disregard of the experience with AFDC by those who favored easy access to food stamps over program integrity is intriguing.

The battle, as it was fought out, involved members of Congress, appointed officials in the Food and Nutrition Service (FNS) of the U.S. Department of Agriculture (USDA), state and local officials charged with administering the program, the courts, and the food-stamp-advocacy groups—Food Research Action Committee (FRAC) and Community Action Legal Services (CALS)—and related advocacy groups. A major role was played by the food stamp advocacy groups working closely with their allies in Congress and in the FNS and with comparable officials at the state and local levels.

In Congress, the differences were not simply politically partisan. Senators Robert Dole, a conservative Republican, and George McGovern, a very liberal Democrat, both from Midwestern farm states, were equally ardent in their support of relatively open access to the program and were joined in the House by Congressman Frederick Richmond, a liberal Democrat from Brooklyn. The food stamp advocacy groups, including lawyers, economists, and other professionals, were technically skilled, very knowledgeable, and dedicated to promoting the broadest possible interpretation of the laws and regulations to achieve increased program participation—no matter what the results were in administrative complexity, costs, and potential errors in determining eligibility or the amount of benefits. They had close working alliances with Arthur Schiff, director of the food stamp program in New York City under the Lindsay administration, with Congressman Richmond, chairman of the House Agriculture Committee's subcommittee on food and nutrition, and, with the advent of the Carter administration in 1977, with Agriculture Secretary Bob Bergland and Assistant Secretary Carol Foreman, who had responsibility for the Food Stamp program. Indeed, Robert Greenstein, who was active in advocacy circles, became a special assistant to Secretary Bergland and later was appointed acting administrator of the FNS. Their main working alliance within New York City was with Carol Bellamy, president of the City Council; one of the CALS staff, Barry Ensminger, joined her staff shortly after she took office in 1978.

The members of the alliance had different motivations for

expanding the food stamp program. Senators Dole and Mc-Govern, as well as other legislators from farm states, wanted to expand the market for farm products to help the farmers. Congressman Richmond and the food stamp advocates were concerned with helping the poor, a concern widely shared by liberals and moderates, and even by conservatives. But the alliance wanted to stretch the law and the regulations to help them more. Ranged against them were three main groups. The first was the administrators of the food stamp program at state and local levels. These officials were under pressure from the governors and legislators to stay within administrative budgets, threatened from time to time, depending on the administration in Washington, by fiscal penalties because of high ineligibility rates, and concerned by the public reaction. The second group was made up of many in Congress who were concerned that administration of the program should not subvert legislative intent. And the third group was the general public, which was becoming increasingly irritated at the evident widespread abuse.

The battle was fully joined in Congress in 1977, when new legislation was under consideration to reform the food stamp program. But before analyzing the debate and its outcome, it is necessary to describe some of the atmosphere and events in the preceding two years inside, as well as outside, the halls of Congress.

THE EMERGING CONFLICT

Since the passage of the original Food Stamp Act, state and local administrators of this complex program have been subjected to conflicting pressures. During 1975–1977, under the Ford administration, the main outcry from FNS officials was over the high rates of ineligibility among nonwelfare food stamp recipients and the excess issuance of stamps to both welfare and nonwelfare groups. Corrective action was the focus of attention. At the same time, FRAC and CALS were instituting lawsuits to remedy what they regarded as unfair treatment of clients who, because of technical complications in the regulations, might not have obtained the full benefits to which they were entitled. Their frequent successes resulted in greatly increased work loads imposed on limited state and local staff members, who were therefore unable to devote sufficient attention to corrective action to reduce ineligibility and overissuance.

This conflict is revealed in the testimony at hearings, held before various committees of the Senate and House in 1975 and 1976, which dealt with issues of program integrity, administrative complexity, and the goals of the program in terms of the income groups to be served.[2] The General Accounting Office was critical of the quality control systems FNS required of the states and stressed the high rate of ineligibility—18 percent of nonwelfare cases in the first half of 1974. USDA officials agreed that the error rate was too high and expressed opposition to proposals to loosen procedures aimed at the verification of eligibility, as did several state officials. But at the same hearing, in April–May 1975, most of the remaining witnesses (who were mainly from advocacy groups) were more concerned with low participation rates than with program integrity. While the failure of states to implement adequate "outreach" programs was the main topic of discussion, some witnesses attacked the certification procedure, urging that it be replaced by a self-declaration method. They were supported in this request by Senators Dole and McGovern, who submitted an amendment described by Dole as "in itself a self-declaration."

Verification is a crucial issue in the argument about the balance to be struck between participation and program integrity and, as we shall see, it was to become a major point of contention surrounding the legislation enacted in 1977 and the federal regulations that followed.

In New York State, and particularly in New York City, the program was under heavy attack from some state legislators and from the advocacy groups for insufficient participation.* It was

---

*The Subcommittee on Nutrition of the New York State Assembly's Committee on Social Services, chaired by Bronx Democrat Estelle Diggs, held

also attacked by Congressman Richmond's subcommittee, which held hearings in February 1977 on the operation of the food stamp program in New York State and New York City.

State and local efforts to increase program participation and the success achieved—an 8.6 percent increase during 1975 and a further 10 percent increase between December 1975 and October 1976—were denigrated by Congressman Richmond, who criticized the small size of the state staff devoted to promoting outreach activities.

The exchange of views at the hearings brought to the fore two sources of the conflict between state and local officials administering the program and those, like Congressman Richmond and the food stamp advocates, whose major, if not sole, concern was its expansion.

The first related to the charge of inadequate staffing. It should be noted that the state does pay 50 percent of the administrative cost of the program. Beginning in the summer of 1975, as the state was preoccupied with the fiscal crisis in New York City, as well as with its own severe fiscal problems, personnel cuts and ceilings were imposed on most state agencies, including NYSDSS. A commissioner did make the cost-benefit argument, but it had limited appeal to harassed budget officials. The second charge stemmed from the notion, favored by advocacy groups, that since the cost of food stamp benefits was borne exclusively by the federal government, state and local officials did not need to worry about ineligibility. But not all, or even a majority, of state and local officials, particularly those in upstate New York, regard federal dollars as manna from heaven. Rather, they regard federal dollars as real money and, indeed,

public hearings in New York City on January 13, 1977, and subsequently issued a report entitled *An Unfulfilled Promise*. One of the authors of the report was Arthur Schiff, who was the food stamp director in the Lindsay administration and at this point was associated with the food stamp advocacy groups. It was no surprise, therefore, that the report excoriated state and local food stamp officials, as did all of the witnesses who represented various community organizations and advocacy groups.

as *their* money—taxes paid by New Yorkers and not tax dollars from Mississippi or Arkansas. Therefore these officials, unlike their critics, feel money from the federal government should be spent carefully and with due regard not only to law and regulation but also to a sense of priority of needs—as if the money came directly from state and local taxes.

Subsequently, in June 1977, Congressman Richmond wrote to Secretary Bergland suggesting administrative reforms based on the hearings. The administrative faults emphasized by the subcommittee provoked a July 1977 letter from J. Henry Smith, then HRA commissioner, to Congressman Richmond, saying that Richmond had ignored the improvements made in program administration during the preceding six months.

THE CONFLICT BETWEEN THE FEDS AND THE STATES

These exchanges over the administration of the food stamp program did not, however, end the matter. To the surprise of state and city officials, on April 18, 1978, USDA released an audit entitled *Food Stamp Operations in New York State,* which was highly critical of the administration of the program in the state, particularly in New York City.

It turned out that the USDA audit was initiated and structured by staff from CALS and FRAC, prepared at the request of Congressman Richmond and five members of his subcommittee and based in substantial measure on the "findings" of the Richmond hearings in February 1977 on food stamp operations in New York City. Christine Van Lanten, acting administrator of FNS, reported in her April 14 letter to Congressman Richmond that Barry Ensminger's efforts in exploring the findings of the Richmond hearings and in helping FNS contact advocacy groups were "invaluable." Congressman Richmond, in concert with City Council President Bellamy (as indicated earlier, Barry Ensminger was a member of her staff) used the report to issue a press release and hold a news conference attacking the administration of the program in the city.

The NYSDSS commissioner, Barbara Blum, and I as HRA commissioner responded on April 20 with a press release which stated that most of the criticisms in the report concerned minor matters and were often blatantly outdated. With respect to the charge that some localities, including New York City, denied recipients their full benefits by using inappropriate standards to determine eligibility, we referred to audits that refuted the allegation that food stamp recipients were, to any significant degree, denied the benefit of all allowable deductions. We also listed other major program improvements made in New York City that USDA chose to overlook.

In sum, we characterized the entire report as "slanted to magnify the impact of minor problems, clearly and admittedly written to ignore program improvements, and released in a spirit of bad faith typical of the insensitivity of USDA to its own shortcomings and the state and local difficulties of administering the program under USDA aegis."* The April 1978 battle of the press releases was only an additional, though acute, manifestation of the corrosion of relations between FNS and New York State and local officials with respect to the administration of the food stamp program.

Lest it be thought that New York was the only state having trouble with USDA, let me hasten to note that this was not so. At a March 2, 1978, meeting of APWA's National Council of State Administrators, in response to the dissatisfaction expressed by many present, Lewis Straus, Administrator of FNS, expressed an interest in improving relationships between USDA and the states. Thus encouraged, John Dempsey, Commissioner of the Michigan Department of Social Services, wrote to Straus shortly thereafter. He indicated that certain FNS practices di-

---

*Nevertheless, Council President Bellamy, through Ensminger, continued her criticism, making detailed recommendations for restructuring the top HRA staff in charge of the food stamp program, for extending the outreach program, despite evidence that the payoff on such efforts had diminished to a low level, and for eliminating various requirements for verification which HRA considered essential to maintain quality control.

rectly prevented the efficient operation of the program in his state and fostered the very operational deficiencies that prompted the warnings of fiscal sanctions so frequently issued by USDA. Moreover, he noted that while Michigan's operational deficiencies were always well documented by USDA, the state's efforts to resolve these problems and the fact that the problems were exacerbated by FNS procedures were often ignored.

According to Commissioner Dempsey, FNS's habit of issuing frequent, untimely policy and procedural changes constituted the most offensive administrative practice. The directives always contained time constraints that simply did not allow for the proper implementation of the procedure or policy in question. On this point, Dempsey wrote: "It is literally impossible for my staff efficiently and effectively to assimilate and implement directives issued in this manner. Because of inadequate lead time given us, program staff in our control office can seldom process changes quickly enough to permit sufficient lead time for training and timely implementation in the field. The net result is a demoralized and frustrated staff working under intolerable conditions." In this connection, he urgently requested FNS not to confuse the administrative problems faced by Michigan with those faced by sparsely populated rural states. On the latter point, he wrote: "When I speak with FNS officials, I'm regularly outraged to be told that we shouldn't have any problems State X doesn't (State X usually being a scarcely populated, western state with a population smaller than Michigan's food stamp caseload alone). I urge you to visit the New Yorks, Illinois, Pennsylvanias, or Michigans of this nation. Such a visit, I'm sure, will convince you that we do have a widespread problem."

THE CONFLICT IN THE COURTS

Court involvement in the interpretation of regulations and administration of the food stamp program is similar to recent court history with respect to a great deal of legislation, regulations, and administration, not only in the social field but in others as well. No one can gainsay the right of citizens to apply to the courts for remedy of apparent wrongs or the courts' right to determine the parameters of their authority. Yet much concern has been expressed in recent years by thoughtful commentators and analysts over the extension of the courts' prerogatives into the minutest details of program administration. A recent example of this expression of concern is an article by Charles Fried, Professor of Law, Harvard Law School, on the Op-Ed page of the *New York Times*, November 10, 1981. He starts by saying, "Federal district judges are increasingly acting as day-to-day managers and implementers, reaching into the details of civic life: how programs are run, medication is administered to the mentally ill, custody is arranged for severely deranged persons, private and public employers recruited and promoted. Though judicial authority and democracy have always coexisted in tension, as Federal judges assume a more active managerial role, politicians and citizens chafe for quite pragmatic reasons."

While it cannot be denied that federal, state, and local welfare agencies are far from perfect, or that by nature a bureaucracy moves slowly and responds reluctantly to change, one must also recognize that it does take an enormous effort to implement major changes in the laws and regulations that govern so complex a program as food stamps. In any major city, hundreds, sometimes several thousands, of staff must be retrained to understand and implement the new regulations and procedures; computers must be reprogrammed (a process filled with hazards and pitfalls); and always all this must be done while the daily business under the old regulations is carried on. The food stamp bureau cannot be closed down during alterations.

How does one draw the line between the protection of a client's rights and the hard realities of administrative complexities in a system that in New York City alone provides food stamps to over 450,000 families, including well over one million persons? If a significant proportion of actual or potential clients is denied benefits altogether or to a substantial degree, clearly the courts, as a matter of justice, must intervene. But does it make sense for the courts to require an enormous and costly administrative effort—costly not only in direct financial expenditures but also in its impact on the effectiveness of administration—to correct minor underissuances of benefits to a small proportion of clients?

A review of all the significant legal cases related to the food stamp program during the last decade is beyond the scope of this book. Yet it is useful to focus on a few cases to clarify the nature of the courts' involvement in the issue of program integrity. In making this review of court cases it is necessary to bear in mind that a public interest law group such as Community Action Legal Services does not only regard its mission to be to expand participation and enlarge the amount of benefits to clients as much as possible, regardless of legislative intent or resulting administrative complexity; it also has considerable freedom in deciding in what locale and before which judge to bring its suit. And, of course, CALS will pick a judge likely to be favorable to its point of view. This may be regarded as a sensible and legitimate action for a law firm to take, but the societal consequences are not necessarily beneficial. This is especially true where the lawyers for the defense—that is, counsel to NYSDSS or HRA—also have more than a touch of the welfare advocate in them. The fact of the matter is that over the last two decades, social service departments in New York, as in other localities, have attracted lawyers whose liberal, humanitarian traditions lead them to view themselves more as lawyers for the welfare or food stamp clients than for the city or state department they serve. Indeed, they see themselves as defenders of the poor against the heartless governmental bureaucracy. Sometimes a commissioner feels bereft of legal counsel, and sometimes he or she is in fact bereft.*

In *Lugo and Hyman* v. *Butz,* a class action suit commenced in the U.S. District Court, Southern District of New York, in

---

*On more than one occasion during my tenure as HRA commissioner, for instance, I found it necessary to remind departmental lawyers that the commissioner—or the City of New York—was their client.

March 1976, the issue derived from conflicting interpretations of the regulations governing the interval between a decision on the client's eligibility and the "prompt" issuance of the authorization to purchase food stamps (known as the ATP). State and city officials argued that prompt action required the ATP to be issued within forty-five days of the initial application or, in other words, within fifteen days after the expiration of the thirty-day maximum period for determination of eligibility. The plaintiffs maintained that the ATP had to be issued within thirty days of the initial application.*

The case was settled by a consent decree which required that retroactive benefits be provided to all households that applied for food stamps between April 1, 1976, and February 28, 1979, received food stamps at some time between December 1, 1978, and February 28, 1979, but did not receive an ATP the month following the month of application. (For example, a person who applied on August 15, 1977, and was accepted on September 15, 1977, became entitled by this decision to benefits for the entire month of September.) In addition, retroactive benefits were to be provided for any months between the month in which the application was accepted and the first month covered by an ATP.

In New York City, according to an affidavit dated December 1979, signed by Herb Rosenzweig, HRA Deputy Com-

---

*The facts of the case are that Mrs. Lugo applied for food stamps for her family on December 22, 1975; the application was approved on January 6, 1976; and the first ATP was issued on January 27, 1976. Specifically, the question was whether or not Mrs. Lugo should have received retroactive benefits for the month of January since she applied on December 22, 1975, received her first ATP on January 27, 1976, and so did not receive any benefits until February 1, 1976, an elapsed time of forty days. Mrs. Hyman's case was more complex, involving some income received, a loan from her sister, misplaced records, a fair hearing (which she won), and unsuccessful efforts to reach her by phone. The issue was whether she was entitled to the retroactive benefits ordered by the fair hearing decision, even though she was no longer eligible for food stamps because of her increased income.

missioner for Income Maintenance, the results of a review to determine retroactive benefits were as follows:

1. 148,572 requests for case file reviews were received.
2. 25,591 households were determined to be eligible for retroactive food stamp benefits amounting to $3.4 million.
3. 122,981 households were determined to be ineligible for retroactive food stamp benefits and were notified of their right to a fair hearing.

Thus a tremendous administrative effort at a cost of $544,000 resulted in additional benefits of $3.4 million to 3 to 4 percent of all households in the city receiving food stamp benefits and added about 0.2 percent to the total benefits received during the three-year period from April 1976 through February 1979.

In *Rivera* v. *U.S. Department of Agriculture* (a case in which NYSDSS and HRA were also named as defendants), tried in the U.S. District Court, Southern District of New York, HRA was charged with errors in calculating food stamp benefits between January 1972 and October 1976, mainly because it did not always make appropriate allowances for all the deductions to which the client might be entitled. A review of records of all households receiving food stamps during this period was requested, with appropriate adjustments for those who had not received their full entitlement. Again, a settlement was reached and a court decree issued.*

In order to satisfy the court order, HRA had to send letters to 450,000 households receiving food stamps in October 1976, asking them whether they felt an error had been made in the amount of benefits received between January 1972 and October 1976 and, if so, requesting information on the date when the

---

*At the time, I was Deputy Commissioner for Income Maintenance at NYSDSS and was appalled when I learned that counsel to the department had agreed to the settlement. I was well aware of the administrative consequences of reviewing the city's food stamp caseload for the preceding five years, but it was too late to reverse the action, and New York City officials had to comply.

error had been made. The total cost of complying with the court's order was approximately $600,000.*

What were the results when the review was completed in October 1977? In summary, $600,000 was spent to provide retroactive benefits for 9,207 households, about 2 percent of all eligible households in 1977. No record of the value of the retroactive benefits is available, but clearly it was a minuscule percentage of the total value of food stamp benefits issued in the more than four-year period.

Aiken v. *Butz* was directed against a USDA regulation rather than administrative failures on the part of HRA, but its impact was similar. In this case, the court struck down a USDA requirement that, pending verification through the usual procedure, at least one collateral contact be made before certification of a case for emergency issuance of food stamps (that is, for a "zero purchase" involving no cash outlay by the client) and limiting such emergency certifications to one in a six-month period. The court settlement agreed to by USDA, without consultation with New York or, apparently, with any other state authorities, required that all households that applied for or even inquired about food stamps from August 5, 1974, to December 31, 1977, and that were denied or received late benefits because the collateral contact could not be completed or because certification prior to verification had already been granted once within the preceding six months, were entitled to retroactive benefits.**

It should be noted that without a collateral contact it becomes extraordinarily easy for anyone to walk into a food stamp

---

*At my urging, counsel to HRA requested and received permission from the court allowing HRA to ignore those letters that said an error had been made but did not indicate the dates when it occurred. The costs would have been substantially more without this modification.

**According to USDA officials, USDA opposed the elimination of the collateral contact but was barred from negotiating the issue with the court, apparently because USDA had not included provision for this in the regulations. Subsequently, USDA reimposed the collateral contact rule by including it in the regulations.

center, claim, for example, that he has no money or resources and has a wife and five children, and, on this declaration, walk out with an authorization to obtain more than $150 in food stamps at no cost. (This issue will come up again in my discussion of the USDA regulations implementing the 1977 food stamp legislation.) NYSDSS Commissioner Barbara Blum wrote to the administrator of FNS in March 1975 that the settlement, "granting relief to a class of people who cannot be identified and about whom no record was retained or required to be retained, undermines any attempt that states are making to bring integrity to the program in terms of quality control."

The cost of implementing the court settlement was $102,000. The results were that, of the 31,000 households contacted, 1,516 responded; 853 of these signed applications for retroactive benefits. Upon examination, it was found that 183 applicants were entitled to benefits totaling $18,776. These figures require no further comment.

While it means getting ahead of the story a little, it is worth discussing one more case—even though it arose as a result of the 1977 legislation. In the course of introducing the Senate-House conference report on the 1977 food stamp bill, Democratic Congressman Thomas Foley of Washington, chairman of the House Agriculture Committee, stated: "Since the passage of the last major program changes in January 1971, well over 100 lawsuits have been brought in every state in the country by attorneys for organizations receiving Federal funds. The intent of Congress was not as explicitly expressed as it might have been in 1969, 1970, and 1971, *but whatever intent there was, has often been distorted in my judgment by the process of litigation"* (italics added). He concluded his comments with respect to the litigation by saying that "lawyers may probe and test every section of this bill to seek soft spots or loopholes. We hope there are none. But if the courts should confront such cases, we trust that they will read and construe this new food stamp law in the light of our intent to trust its management to the Department of Agriculture operating in good faith and under the guidance of the legislative dictates." Foley's trust was not altogether misplaced with respect to lawsuits on the national level, but it was with respect to local lawsuits in New York.

The Food Stamp Act of 1977 replaced the variety of allowable deductions from gross income with a standard deduction. It was estimated that the new requirements would reduce benefits to some welfare recipients and increase them to others, in both instances in amounts up to $10 per month. It was also estimated that some public assistance households receiving income from work, as well as welfare, would become ineligible for food stamps because total income would exceed eligibility limits.

To implement this aspect of the law, HRA's Division of Income Maintenance sent a letter to all food stamp recipients on welfare, advising them of the changes in the law and indicating that, as a result, their food stamp benefits might go up or down by as much as $10 per month. The letter did not, however, provide a detailed calculation for each household, showing how the new benefit level was determined, a procedure agreed to by USDA and NYSDSS to lighten the work load added to the already heavy administrative burden of implementing the new regulations.

CALS quickly brought suit on behalf of Hilda Rodriguez and all other public assistance households whose benefits were reduced or terminated (*Rodriguez* v. *Bernstein*). The plaintiffs claimed that due process of law was violated because they were not advised of the precise calculation underlying the change in the grant. They originally sought a return to the March 1, 1979, status quo for all recipients whose benefits were reduced or terminated prior to the court-required issuances of new notices to clients detailing the basis of the change in benefits. The court denied this request for preliminary relief because city officials effectively argued that a rollback would paralyze HRA. It was one of the few times a court gave some recognition to administrative problems, but apparently nothing short of paralysis will elicit the courts' concern.

In the opinion of counsel to the city and the state, as well as USDA, HRA would in the end have lost the case, and thus negotiations were entered into for settlement. The arrangement required HRA to mail a notice to all 330,000 public assistance households advising them of the data on file on which the calculation of food stamp benefits was based and enclosing a worksheet that would permit the household to make its own calculation. The notice further advised them that if they considered HRA to have made an error, they could consult an income maintenance worker and that if they requested a fair hearing, their March 1 benefit would be restored, and they would receive retroactive benefits back to March 1, 1979. Costs incurred in implementing the settlement came to about $135,000; about 300 households requested fair hearings, of which half obtained continuing aid at the previous level, or about $5,000 in additional benefits.

The four cases cited, which are a reasonable sample of the types of suits brought by CALS in recent years, have some important common characteristics. The cost-benefit ratio has been dismal, the proportion of food stamp recipients involved is small, and the amount of additional benefits paid out as a proportion of total benefits even smaller. The additional administrative burden has been heavy, particularly in cases involving retroactive review over a period of years, and the government always loses. Further, the cost figure in the cost-benefit equation does not, by any stretch of the imagination or by any realistic accounting, measure the full costs of the involvement of top food stamp staff in these full-time distractions from the effort to improve the management of the program. As a result, the quality of services to clients suffered at least as much as program integrity.

THE FOOD STAMP ACT OF 1977

Officials in New York State and New York City remained under constant attack from FNS, Congressman Richmond, and the advocacy groups during 1977 and into 1978 for what was regarded as inadequate outreach, inadequate staffing, excessive verification, and overconcern about recipients' eligibility. At the same time, in response to the mounting costs of the program and the widespread belief that it was rife with fraud and abuse, Congress began to debate the bill that was to become the Food Stamp Act of 1977.

Among the major features of the bill, perhaps the most significant was the elimination of the purchase price for food stamps. Previously, those eligible were permitted to purchase enough food stamps to provide an adequate diet; the amount of stamps was determined in relation to the size of the family or household unit. The difference between the purchase price and the face value of the stamps was the "bonus" or subsidy. It was generally believed that the need to put up a significant amount of cash to obtain the bonus discouraged some eligible recipients from taking advantage of the benefits. There were administrative reasons as well for eliminating the purchase price and providing only the bonus; it greatly reduced the volume of food stamps distributed, eliminated the necessity for food stamp distributors to handle large amounts of cash, and significantly reduced accounting reconciliation problems.

It was anticipated that elimination of the purchase price would substantially expand participation of eligible persons in the program, and this anticipation was realized. (What was not realized, and perhaps should have been, was that eliminating the purchase price would also, as discussed below, expand participation of ineligible persons in the program.) Since the goal of the bill was to hold costs at the existing level of about $6 billion, the expected increase in participation was to be counterbalanced by lowering the net income eligibility limit to the poverty line (about $1,000 below the existing eligibility level) and by replacing a variety of allowable deductions with a standard deduction, which included $60 for all families, 20 percent of earned income, and a maximum of $75 a month for excess shelter costs and/or child-care expenses.

In combination with the net income eligibility level, the standard deduction served to set a gross income ceiling on the program for the first time and was designed to eliminate eligibility for middle-income families. Further, limitations were put on the eligibility of college students to eliminate what had been regarded as one of the more irritating abuses of the program, even though students never constituted more than 2 percent of all recipients. In addition, eligibility would no longer be automatic for welfare recipients but would be related to their total income from welfare and work. Methods of determining eligibility were to be tightened up; the bill did not specify the mechanism, leaving this to the discretion of the Secretary of Agriculture.

Various senators—mainly Republicans and Southern Democrats—sought amendments that would strengthen the verification process. For example, Republican Senator Carl Curtis of Nebraska offered amendments that would have required food stamp recipients to use photo ID cards and would have established a system to cross-check claimed income with available wage reporting systems. Both were voted down. It was not until 1980 that states were allowed the option of using a photo ID system (excluding, however, aged and disabled recipients) and checking with a wage reporting system was permitted.

Some senators, such as the late Senator Hubert Humphrey of Minnesota, emphasized the importance of avoiding program cutbacks and ensuring that food stamps were available to all eligible persons. And Senator Dick Clark, Democrat of Iowa, indicated that while the fraud provisions must be enforced, it should not be at the cost of excessive verification or of a slowdown in the provision of benefits.

In summarizing the compromise bill adopted by the Senate-House Conference Committee, Congressman Foley indicated that a number of amendments offered during the earlier House debate, designed to improve program integrity, had been voted down either by the House itself or in the conference committee. Nevertheless, the introduction to the report of the House Agriculture Committee stated that the act is a "tightly interrelated package of provisions that accomplishes several major objectives." The objectives were listed as "simplifying and tightening program administration, facilitating access to the program for eligible and potentially eligible households, eliminating households with high gross income, and reducing the potential for errors and program fraud and abuse."

THE DRAFT REGULATIONS: DID THEY ACHIEVE THEIR OBJECTIVES?

Regulations should simply provide for the technical application of congressional legislative intent. In recent years, however, regulations have often made policy and not just carried it out. How well did the draft regulations prepared by USDA after the Food Stamp Act was passed achieve each of the objectives in the 1977 amendments, and how was the balance struck between accessibility and program integrity? One brief response is to say that when they were circulated for comment, the regulations created consternation among state and local administrators, eliciting from them long, detailed, and highly critical reactions. On the other hand, the regulations were generally applauded by community and advocacy groups. But the question merits further consideration.

The position of officials in New York City was presented in my letter of June 21, 1978, as HRA commissioner to Nancy Snyder, director of FNS Food Stamp Division. We were critical of the draft regulations, though we strongly supported both the overall goals of the food stamp program as a vital income support measure and the two major provisions of the 1977 act: the elimination of the purchase price and the standardization of deductions. My letter recognized that administrative procedures designed to prevent fraud could stifle participation and delay the provision of assistance, but also that procedures aimed at quick access could open the door to potential fraud and abuse. I added, "We must find a way to walk the middle road between these two extremes."

In our view, the proposed regulations did not strike an effective compromise between the two goals because they placed dangerous restrictions on the local agency's ability to verify client eligibility and to terminate benefits for noncompliance with the regulations. Specifically, under the proposed regulations, local agencies would be permitted to verify only nonexempt gross income, utility expenses (if a client claimed a deduction in excess of the standard deductions), and alien status. Egregious omissions from the list of verifiable items included family size and assets. Benefit levels depend on both, and I said of their omission: "I feel that this is an open invitation to fraud." How important these factors are can be understood from the difference in benefits, for example, between a two-person and a four-person family—$86 per month. Liquid assets of more than $1,750 made a family ineligible for any benefits.

In effect, the determination of eligibility was to be based largely on a self-declaration, despite the well-known, disastrous experience with the use of this method in the AFDC program. Further, under then current regulations in the food stamp program in New York City, 35 percent of the cases who were neither on welfare nor receiving Supplemental Security Income (SSI) were found to be ineligible, mainly because they provided incorrect information on their earnings, family size, and assets. We were concerned that as a result of inadequate verification, an aura of maladministration and fraud would inevitably shroud the food stamp program, and, of course, that the state and local administrations would get most of the blame and be threatened by USDA with fiscal sanctions. I wrote that the descriptive material in the draft regulations stated, "The Act provides that nonexempt gross income must be verified along with such other eligibility factors as the Secretary determines necessary," and I added, "We believe that it is necessary for the state and localities to have the authority to require verification of all items affecting eligibility and benefits levels. We strongly urge you to revise the proposed regulations accordingly."

We also took serious exception to the proposed regulations affecting expedited services. Local agencies were limited to verifying nonexempt income and to making a collateral contact to establish an applicant's identity and place of residence. Further, verification of a client's statement that he had no income was permitted only within so limited a period that it was not generally possible to accomplish it. To illustrate the potential result of these restrictions, a man could walk into a certifying center, tell the worker that he had lost his job, had no income, and had a wife and five children. After the worker checked with the collateral contact, who said the man was "John Smith" and did live at the address he had given, John Smith could walk out with $286 in food stamps. I urged that "the localities should be allowed to develop a workable and administratively feasible way to assure the timely delivery of service to persons in need."

The third major criticism of the draft regulations related to the recertification interview, an essential element in the procedure for assuring continued eligibility to receive food stamps. Under the old rules, if a client did not appear for a scheduled interview and did not call to explain and request another appointment, the case could be closed after due notification. Indeed, many were closed on this basis, and in at least half the cases nothing further was heard from the recipients; it was reasonable to assume they no longer needed food stamps. The draft regulations appeared to permit the closing of a case only for refusal to be interviewed and not for failure to keep or reschedule the appointment. And they could be construed as prohibiting the agency from terminating benefits if the client failed to respond to letters rescheduling recertification appointments. Therefore, once accepted for service, clients could be assured of continuing to receive food stamps as long as they never answered mail sent by the agency—in effect, never overtly refusing to be interviewed, just failing to respond or appear. In terms of effective administration of the program and prompt attention to clients without their waiting hours to be interviewed, it was essential to schedule appointments. We therefore urged that the final regulations permit the local agency to send clients a closing notice if they failed to respond to a call-in for recertification.

The city's criticisms of the draft regulations were supported by New York State officials in a June 16, 1978, letter from Sydelle

Shapiro, NYSDSS Deputy Commissioner, to Nancy Snyder. In particular, they noted that the draft regulations incorporated "a nearly self-declaration certification process into the program" and that an applicant who claimed an emergency and requested immediate issuance must be given the stamps even without income verification. They agreed that such a certification process would expedite the provision of food stamps and believed that the vast majority of clients would not misinform food stamp officials, but they noted, *"USDA must be aware, however, that quality control results will suffer"* (italics in original). The state also shared the view of HRA officials with respect to the recertification process and urged a change in the regulations to permit local agencies to close a case, on due notification, for failure to cooperate with the agency when the client did not telephone or keep the interview appointment.

The draft regulations with respect to the self-declaration method and verification procedures for regular and emergency cases elicited critical comments in their letters to FNS not only from New York officials, but from many other states as well. Michigan, in particular, which has many of the same problems as New York (Detroit is very similar to New York City), protested vigorously. Pennsylvania and Massachusetts, along with New York, suggested that if the self-declaration method were to be used, errors resulting from it should not be counted against the states. The Michigan reply suggested mildly that "the verification requirements are extremely liberal." Massachusetts, Michigan, and Illinois objected strenuously to the provisions regarding expedited service. The Illinois reply stated, "The administrative prerogative taken by FNS staff in this section is outlandish and indefensible." Several states, including California, Massachusetts, and Pennsylvania, were as concerned as New York with what they interpreted as a prohibition on closing cases for failure to cooperate and permitting it only for refusal to cooperate.

Considerable ire was also directed against the draft regulation setting staffing standards for bilingual workers. It required an interpreter to be available to all food stamp centers for every language spoken by at least 150 non-English-speaking low-income households in an area apparently defined (this was unclear) as a city or county. In New York City, of course, such a regulation would create an administrative nightmare, as it would in several other urban centers. This provision constituted the most egregious effort by USDA to impose central control on cities throughout the country in order to ensure participation in the program without regard to administrative cost or feasibility. HRA suggested that the worthy goal of ensuring access of non-English-speaking clients could be achieved by providing Spanish interpreters at all food stamp centers and interpreters for all other languages at one specified site in the city.

But while state and local administrators were critical of the draft regulations, Congressman Richmond and the food stamp advocacy groups defended them. Richmond wrote to Assistant Agriculture Secretary Foreman on August 16, 1978, describing my letter of June 21 as full of "errors and incorrect interpretation of the regulations." Actually, his letter confirmed the city's criticism of the limited verification permitted in the draft regulations. He charged the state and city with following a policy of requiring verification of every factor relating to eligibility (in fact, family size and assets were verified) and characterized it as one of the major barriers to participation in the food stamp program in New York. He then made the curious argument that, under the new law, very few persons other than those receiving welfare, SSI, or social security benefits would be eligible for food stamps and that, therefore, complete verification would already have been done in checking eligibility for public assistance and SSI.

Richmond's prediction that eligibility for nonwelfare cases would be virtually eliminated turned out to be thoroughly wrong. Nonwelfare food stamp recipients constituted more than one-third (37 percent) of the total in June 1980, compared with only 27 percent in December 1978. SSI recipients accounted for only about one-fifth of the increase. HRA's quality control study for the period from October 1979 through March 1980 showed that the highest client error rate (38.8 percent) occurred among nonwelfare, non-SSI cases; in a memorandum dated October 30, 1980, Herb Rosenzweig, HRA Deputy Administrator for Income Maintenance, attributed the high error rate to USDA regulations which "do not allow us to verify information provided by the client on eligibility factors such as household composition and utility deductions."

The final regulations implementing the Food Stamp Act of 1977 were issued in October 1978. USDA did respond positively to state and local government complaints about time schedules for implementation of the regulations and about some particularly horrendous administrative complexities, but USDA also gave substantial weight to comments and criticism from advocacy groups intent on quick implementation of the law and detailed provisions protecting clients' rights. In particular, USDA, to accommodate the states' requests that it stagger the implementation of various sections of the act, required them to eliminate the purchase price as of January 1, 1979, but to postpone the replacement of the variety of individual deductions by the standard deduction until March 1, 1979. Thus the provisions designed to increase program participation were implemented two months before those designed to eliminate families above the new, lower income eligibility criteria. This decision, of course, involved a substantial additional cost and was one of the reasons the budget ceiling for the food stamp program was pierced. The new provisions could have been implemented in reverse order, but the advocacy groups insisted that the elimination of the purchase price be given priority. Several congressmen were indignant about the matter and made their views known at various committee hearings.

Some compromise is evident with respect to the issue of verification, but no significant changes were made with respect to expedited services. Under the final regulations, the assets, as well as the income, of a regular applicant for food stamps can be verified if state agencies "feel there is need." New York State feels this way. But the size of the household, a critical element in determining benefits, can be verified only if the food stamp applicant is also a public assistance applicant or recipient. The nonwelfare applicant can simply declare the size of the family without providing any verification, and the statement cannot be challenged or verified by the local agency. Furthermore, while income can be verified by requesting copies of income tax returns or salary check stubs, it cannot be checked against wage reporting records available in most states or against unemployment insurance and other benefit records.

No changes were made in the verification requirements for expedited service; beyond verifying identity and residence through a collateral contact, only income can be verified. If applicants claim they have no income, however, benefits cannot be denied because of lack of verification. Applicants claiming an emergency situation must be interviewed within forty-eight hours and, if apparently eligible largely on the basis of a self-declaration, must receive authorization to obtain food stamps within seventy-two hours.

With respect to recertification, the language of the final regulation retains the distinction between refusal and failure to cooperate in the recertification interview. But it does say that if clients fail to appear for the interview without good cause, they lose their right to uninterrupted benefits. HRA has interpreted this section as requiring no change in its past procedure of sending a closing notice if the client fails to appear at the interview and does not call for another appointment. It closes the case if there is no response to the closing notice. USDA is aware of HRA procedures and has not protested this interpretation.

The requirements for bilingual staff were retained in the final regulations, despite all the protests from state administrators. Indeed, they were made more stringent. Bilingual staff are required if there are 100 (instead of 150) low-income single-language non-English-speaking households in the area; as in the draft regulation, state agencies are required to make a survey to estimate the number of households needing bilingual services. HRA attempted a survey, but it proved unsuccessful in eliciting useful information. In response to an earlier court case, however, HRA has stationed Spanish-speaking workers in all its welfare centers and Russian- or Chinese-speaking workers in selected centers. USDA has not made a major issue of the matter, but, of course, it is always possible that CALS will bring a class action suit.

I have not dwelled on the provisions relating to penalties for client fraud and abuse. Suffice it to say that they were, on the whole, weak and, in terms of the real world, contradictory. With respect to fraud, the level for required prosecution was lowered from $400 to $35, an empty threat since it was impossible to persuade local prosecutors to undertake cases involving even $400, and the alternative established in the regulations for administrative fraud hearings was unwieldly and not cost-effective. Short of bringing fraud cases to court, the penalties for abuse are minor and, in effect, nonexistent.

FRAC's *Guide to the Food Stamp Program,* published in July 1979, is instructive on this point. It explains that "making a mistake or forgetting to tell the food stamp office something" relevant to benefit levels is not fraud, and that if benefits are reduced when the information becomes known, the client can request a fair hearing. It goes on to say that if the fair hearing decision is adverse to the client, he or she may be asked to repay the excess stamps received. The guide advises: *"You only have to pay back the stamps if you want to* [italics in original]. If you decide you cannot afford to repay, or do not want to, the food stamp office is not allowed to cut you off the food stamp program, fail to recertify you if you are eligible, or reduce your benefits in any way." With respect to the fraud hearing (also conducted under the auspices of the local agency, not the courts), food stamp recipients are advised: "You don't have to answer their questions or even show up at the hearing. Remember, it is not enough for them to just show that you got too many food stamps, or got stamps when you were not eligible. They must *prove* that you committed fraud." That is, it must be proved that the client deliberately took action knowing it was wrong. The client is also advised that even if he is found guilty, the penalty is not severe; it amounts to disqualification from the program for three months and a request to repay the stamps fraudulently obtained. Again, the guide advises, "You only have to repay if you want to." Only a court decision could disqualify the recipients for as much as six to twenty-four months and require them to repay the excess benefits. But, as indicated, prosecutors are too overburdened to bring to court any but major cases involving large sums of money.

The answer to the question posed at the beginning of this section—how was the balance struck in USDA's regulations between integrity and access?—has to be that it was substantially weighted against integrity and in favor of access. This was a deliberate decision and explains the degree of detail in the regulations as well as their substance. In general, it must be said that the regulations showed little awareness of the varying problems in different areas of the country. In particular, they did not take into account the greater propensity to manipulate a program providing substantial benefits among those living in large urban areas, which provide a high degree of anonymity, as compared to those living in smaller cities and rural areas. There was no response to Commissioner Dempsey's cry: Don't tell me about State X which has a total population about the size of the food stamp caseload in Michigan; consider New York, Illinois, and Michigan.

The twin objectives of the Food Stamp Act of 1977 were to improve access to the program for eligible families and individuals and to improve program integrity, within a budget ceiling established for fiscal 1979 at $6.2 billion. To what extent did the act and the USDA regulations achieve these objectives? The ink was scarcely dry and implementation barely under way when it became clear that participation had indeed expanded, more rapidly and much more than expected. The budget ceiling had to be lifted substantially to avoid an abrupt cessation of the program for several months. While fraud and abuse declined slightly, they remained at high levels—12.6 percent of the dollar value of food stamps issued from October 1979 through March 1980, compared with 13.4 percent from January through June 1978.

The Aftermath of the Regulations

As early as April 25, 1979, Thomas McBride, Inspector General of USDA, said in testimony before a subcommittee of the Senate Committee on Appropriations that his department was concerned about many facets of the program. "The first is the inadequate verification of recipient eligibility information and the related problem of recipient fraud." He also described a new potential for increased fraud as a result of the elimination of the purchase price. Many states send authorizations to purchase food stamps to clients through the mail. The program has always been plagued by clients who falsely reported that the original authorization was lost in the mail or stolen; in these circumstances, they would receive a duplicate and then redeem both. The problem was irritating but not of major consequence when a significant amount of cash had to be put up to obtain the bonus. But once the purchase price was eliminated, the volume of claims of lost or stolen authorizations vastly increased.

In 1978 in New York City, in response to urging from USDA, HRA instituted a procedure whereby clients who claimed their authorization was lost or stolen received a replacement the same day it was requested, instead of after an interval to allow a check to see if the original had been redeemed. As a result, the volume of requests for replacements doubled between March and December 1978, from 5,500 per month to 11,000. Between January and September 1979, after the purchase price was eliminated, the volume more than doubled again, reaching 25,000 requests per month for replacements. The estimated annual loss in illegal replacements was estimated at $18 million. It should be noted that the intelligence system operating among food stamp and welfare clients is quick, easy, and effective. Only late in 1980 was HRA able to develop a rapid reconciliation process to check claims of loss; the immediate effect was to reduce fraudulent replacements to 20 percent of the previous level, at a saving of over $1 million per month.

The projected costs of the program envisaged in the Food Stamp Act turned out to be vastly underestimated, as became evident early in 1979. According to the act, increased costs were to be offset by an appropriate reduction in monthly benefits, but this was never ordered by USDA. Therefore, in the absence of any congressional action, adherence to the ceiling would have meant a complete shutdown of the program for at least two months. A shutdown would indeed have meant severe hardship for the millions of participants, including those on welfare, and had to be avoided. As USDA had gambled it would, Congress raised the ceiling for fiscal 1979 from $6.2 billion to $6.8 billion and permitted the use of an additional $300 million from unspent 1978 funds. Late in 1979, it became evident that the $6.2 billion ceiling set for fiscal 1980 and 1981 would also be insufficient. As a result, amendments adopted in the Food Stamp Act of 1980 raised the ceilings to $9.5 billion and $9.7 billion, respectively. Because of worsening economic conditions, even the new ceilings were more than $1 billion short of what was needed to fund the program fully.

Various explanations have been offered for the large degree of underestimation. According to officials in the USDA and the Congressional Budget Office, it resulted mainly from the unanticipated high rate of inflation in food prices and the rapid increase in participation, which exceeded projections. Despite the legitimacy of this explanation, USDA officials nevertheless began to offer various proposals for improving program integrity by tightening procedures for verifying clients' eligibility and strengthening the provisions with respect to fraud. They also proposed to penalize states that did not reduce their error rates—still refusing to recognize that it was USDA regulations and not the states' administrative ineptness that were mainly responsible for the high error rates.

The atmosphere was changing, however; burgeoning participation and mounting costs forced consideration of serious methods for reducing ineligibility and overissuance. Secretary Bergland, for example, testifying on June 5, 1979, before Congressman Richmond's subcommittee, supported a House bill that would grant the secretary authority to require food stamp recipients to provide their social security numbers to enable agencies to "track through computers the income earned and reported through the Social Security System." Even former food stamp advocate Robert Greenstein, at this point acting administrator of FNS, emphasized the value of using social security numbers and giving states access to social security wage reports and unemployment insurance records. He also underscored the importance of prohibiting defrauders from participating in the program until they had made restitution of all funds fraudulently obtained. The period 1979–1980 was also marked by some improvement in relations between the federal agencies and the states, as federal officials became more understanding of state problems.

Amendments to the Food Stamp Act adopted in 1979 made a client's provision of a social security number a mandatory condition for eligibility; provided states with an incentive for tracking down fraud by permitting them to retain half the funds recouped as a result of the prosecutions; and compelled clients to repay all funds fraudulently obtained as a condition for reestablishing eligibility. Though procedures reflecting the 1979 amendments were not fully in place in all states by the following year, the payment-error rate did decline to 11.2 percent in the country as a whole during April through September 1980, compared with 12.6 percent in the previous semiannual period. It is still excessive. In New York City, the payment-error rate also declined from 25 percent but remained at the high level of 21.7 percent. New York State was 18.3 percent; Michigan, 13.0 percent; Illinois, 11.1 percent.[3]

Congress, in the 1979 amendments, however, had not yet permitted verification of household size and other items; the Senate wanted them, but the House Agriculture Committee did not support the proposal because "there was no particular evidence of need for such broad authority, which might place excessively burdensome demands on applicants and clog the application system without achieving much in the way of cost saving."[4] It took another year to convince the committee.

The House report on its bill, which revised the 1980 Senate bill, described the completion of the change in congressional attitudes. The introductory section essentially stated that program integrity would no longer be sacrificed to enhance participation. It pointed out that in a time of inflation, Americans were more concerned than ever that the needy achieve a nutritionally adequate diet, but that they would no longer tolerate the abuses and waste permeating the Food Stamp program.

In a comment that must have irritated most state and local administrators, the report stated that the new provisions with respect to verification "should end the misperception of many state officials that their hands are tied in connection with verification." It was not a misperception, as two years of experience had so clearly shown. The report did, however, express the realization that many administrative errors had been caused by the constant change in regulations that characterized the last five years of the program's existence. It added, "The states were understandably at the end of their patience with our unsettling method of repealing our mandates before they have even begun to be enforced."

At long last, the 1980 amendments permitted states to verify household size, whether it appeared "questionable" or not, as well as assets and deductions claimed for rent, utilities, and child-care costs. Other factors may also be verified, although this provision is circumscribed by requiring proof that these factors have indeed been responsible for a significant number of errors. With respect to expedited service, the new rules required that income be verified if it was possible to do so within the time limits and, for the first time, allowed the states to verify the applicant's statement that he has no income. The 1980 amendments also permitted computer cross-checking of the food stamp payment files with income tax returns and the files for social security and other benefit payments and provided the legal foundation for state access to these files. They also gave states the option of using photo IDs within certain limits.

Although the 1980 amendments were signed into law on May 16, 1980, USDA did not issue the final regulations implementing them until January 13, 1981. Further, the states and localities were allowed up to 120 days to put changes into effect. Thus the impact on ineligibility and overpayments did not begin to be felt until the late spring of 1981, and data measuring the impact will not be available until well into 1982.

One may ask why did it take Congress and USDA so long to do what obviously needed to be done? The sad experience with the self-declaration in the AFDC program had been well known and documented for some years. The usefulness of the social security number as an identifier to permit cross-checking with other sources of information on family income and public benefits was equally well known. Data were available on the significant savings achieved in the AFDC program in many states and localities and particularly in New York City.

The explanation of why the food stamp program was messed up for so long lies in the triumph of a combination of special interest groups, the food stamps advocacy organizations, and their supporters in Congress from the farm states. They did not want a tight administration of the program because that meant a decline in participation. They were aided and abetted by liberal legislators and by sympathetic officials in the Food and Nutrition Service who were more concerned during this period with providing assistance to the poor than with the adverse public reaction to significant fraud and abuse. The influence of advocacy groups on the legislative process in the past is illustrated by a statement by Jeff Kirsch of FRAC in the *New York Times* (May 26, 1981), in a story on the dwindling influence of liberal lobbyists. He is quoted as saying, "If we didn't have access to key decision makers we had access to people who did have access. The staff not only provided us with input into the decision making process, we used to work very closely with them. The Senate Nutrition Committee staff, for instance, used to act as a sort of in-house lobby for anti-hunger concern." He sadly noted that the situation had changed in 1981.

There is a clear consensus in the country in favor of the food stamp program, for providing an adequate level of nutrition to those unable to obtain it through their own efforts. But the majority are concerned not only to serve the needy, but to do so with reasonable effectiveness and efficiency, as well as compassion. This consensus has been thwarted during the last five years. A counter-reaction set in and the program became a target for budget cuts.

WHAT OF THE FUTURE?

The Reagan administration, as part of its overall budget-reduction plan, recommended a 14 percent cut in anticipated outlays for the food stamp program for fiscal 1982, or a drop of $1.8 billion nationwide from the anticipated level of $12.6 billion based on current law and regulation. One might have hoped for a dispassionate analysis and debate of the proposals, one not based on the assumption of the sanctity of all current benefits or the virtue of all the proposed cuts. The debate can hardly be described as dispassionate, since the supporters of the current program prophesied the return of widespread malnutrition in the country if any cuts were made, and its detractors tried for even deeper cuts than proposed by the President. Nor can the budget reconciliation process in the Congress be described as orderly. Nevertheless, a compromise was reached which results in a slightly lower reduction in costs than the President had asked for—somewhat under $1.7 billion instead of $1.8 billion—and changes were made in specific recommendations. Some analysis of the original recommendations and the final congressional decision, accepted by the administration, reveals that the compromise was not altogether unreasonable.

Part of the Reagan administration's proposed reduction in costs stemmed from improved management and monitoring to ensure compliance with the eligibility requirements. Congress accepted this objective and strengthened potential enforcement techniques by extending the penalty for disqualification from eligibility to include misrepresentation and concealment or withholding of facts, as well as intentional fraud. The penalty period has been increased, and excess payments can to some extent be recovered. Congress anticipates that since the local agency will not need to prove fraud in court, greater use will be made of the more flexible administrative hearing procedures. (FRAC will have to revise its *Guide to the Food Stamp Program.*) Congress also adopted certain technical changes in the definition of a family for purposes of food stamp eligibility (such as eliminating boarders from the family unit); these changes will result in cost savings.

Another recommendation involving significant savings, that benefits begin from the date of application rather than from the beginning of the month in which application was made, was also accepted by Congress without much controversy. The current procedure, after all, reflected a court decision in a suit brought by CALS, rather than congressional intent.

The remaining proposals were all highly controversial. Perhaps the most controversial was the recommendation to reduce food stamp benefits to families whose children are in school and eligible for free school lunches; such lunches are planned to provide one-third of the child's daily nutritional requirement. This recommendation to eliminate the overlap between food stamp benefits and free school lunches accounted for a substantial part of the savings in the Reagan package, roughly 20 to 25 percent. It is difficult to argue against the proposal on the basis of principle; if the goal of adequate nutrition is met by the food stamp allotment, how can one defend a high priority for food benefits in excess of the goal? Nevertheless, the proposal (which was a favorite of Republican Senator Jesse Helms of North Carolina, a tobacco state), was under heavy attack as denying needed benefits to the poorest of the poor. The more persuasive argument, to my mind, lay in the administrative complexity, feasibility, and costs of implementing such a proposal, whether one tried to accomplish it by a monthly adjustment of the family's food stamp allotment or by requiring that school lunches be paid for in food stamps from the family's allotment. In the compromise worked out, the proposal was dropped; the unrealized savings were compensated for in part by lowering eligibility standards for free school lunches and revising other provisions in the food stamp bill designed to achieve additional economies.

Another source of savings lay in the Reagan proposal to repeal certain enrichments in the program provided for in the 1980 amendments and scheduled to come into effect in 1982. In particular, the provision requiring food stamp allotments to be based on projected price changes for food and certain items deductible from income, instead of on actual price changes during a preceding period for which data were available, was to be eliminated. The 1980 amendments had already shifted the semi-annual indexing for price change to an annual basis. It should be noted that what was being proposed was the same system followed with respect to social security payments and many union wage contracts. It does, of course, put a squeeze on recipients during the year as prices rise, but in this respect food stamp recipients would be in no worse a position than social security beneficiaries and most wage earners.

In the final compromise, the principle of annual adjustments based on actual price changes during the preceding period was accepted both for the food stamp allotment and for allowable deductions from income. But an extra squeeze was imposed in the process of shifting from a calendar to a federal fiscal year. Adjustments in the cost of the thrifty food plan, the basis for the food stamp allotment, are delayed until April 1982, July 1983, October 1984, and every October thereafter. The prolongation of the periods between indexing is quite clearly solely a cost-saving device—a compromise to offset the savings foregone with respect to school lunches. It puts an extra burden on families with preschool children, or children no longer in school, and on single individuals, including the aged and disabled. It would be straining matters to try to justify it as good social policy or even as necessary for purposes of federal budgeting by fiscal years. Reagan had also recommended eliminating automatic indexing for cost-of-living changes for certain deductions from income used in determining benefits—again a simple cost-cutting device without social policy justification. In the compromise adopted, indexing of standard or special deductions is postponed until July 1, 1983, October 1, 1984, and every October thereafter.

Also controversial was the proposal to reimpose a cap on gross income limits for food stamp eligibility and place it at 130 percent of the poverty level by not permitting other than standardized deductions; this proposal was accepted by Congress except for the elderly and disabled, who will still be allowed to deduct high rent or medical costs. In effect, eligibility is cut off at about $11,000 for the four-person family. It is not unreasonable to standardize deductions; a rough equity is achieved and administrative complexities are greatly reduced. But the savings involved in lowering the cap are relatively small, and injustice is done to the low-income working poor. A higher cap, one closer to the BLS lower-level living standard ($14,393 in the New York area in autumn 1980 prices, and $14,044 in the country as a whole) would have been more equitable.

The group which has perhaps been most unfairly dealt with in the 1981 amendments is strikers; I refer here to persons engaged in a legal strike in a legitimate labor dispute. Under the new legislation, strikers are barred from eligibility even if they have neither income nor assets. The exception is persons who were receiving food stamps at the time they went on strike, and for them, reduced income is not taken into account. This can hardly be regarded as an illustration of government evenhandedness in a labor dispute.

The Reagan proposal for determining eligibility on the basis of income in a recent period prior to application, rather than in the prospective period, is an issue that has been debated in Congress for some years. In my view, it makes little sense to look to previous income if the income is no longer available. The basis for the proposal is the suspicion, possibly well founded, that the recently unemployed worker has savings on which to draw for at least some period of time. But savings are taken care of by the assets test. What is needed is better enforcement of this test, rather than a delay in providing benefits to the worker who has greatly reduced income or no income at all and who has no savings. Congress approved the proposal but did not mandate its use until October 1, 1983, so there is time for reflection.

Finally, in the light of the earlier discussion of outreach and requirements for bilingual workers, it is worth noting that the requirement for outreach efforts was eliminated on the ground that the mandate was onerous and that the current wide participation in the program is a fair indication that eligible people are well informed about it. States may engage in outreach, if they wish, but federal funding for any outreach program which states may decide to undertake is prohibited. Requirements for bilingual workers are also eliminated, but in this case, if states decide bilingual workers are needed, federal funds will be made available on the usual matching basis. Hallelujah! What could be more reasonable?

How, then, can the impact of the changes proposed by President Reagan and modified by Congress be summed up? Overall, a 13.4 percent cut has been imposed on the program level anticipated for 1982. If one divides up the cuts enacted into law into those which have been described above as reasonable, those described as harsh, and those I consider neutral, the figures are as shown on the following page.[5] For the country as a whole, it appears that about 40 percent of the savings will be achieved from reasonable cuts and 56.8 percent from harsh reductions. The remaining 3.2 percent I can only describe as neutral. The ratio will vary, of course, among different areas depending on the particular mix of the locality's food stamp caseload. It is unlikely, however, to vary enormously.

The Reagan administration justifies the "harsh" cuts in terms of the general necessity for reducing federal expenditures in order to achieve a balanced budget by 1984. This remains an area for public policy debate in the future. But the outcome of that debate, whether it will tend toward the elimination of the harsher cuts or not, will depend to a significant degree on whether program integrity is, in fact, improved while reasonable access is maintained.

	DOLLAR SAVINGS (in millions)
Reasonable	
Improved management (including elimination of outreach)	29
Definition of family and elimination of boarders	60
Repeal of enriched deductions (which never went into effect)	63
Initiation of pro rata benefits	495
Total	*647*
Harsh	
Elimination of benefits to strikers	50
Reduction in gross income limit to 130 percent of poverty level	110
Postponement of indexing of standard deduction and elimination of excess shelter allowance	242
Three-month lag in indexing thrifty food standard	512
Total	*914*
Neutral	
Decrease in earned income deduction from 20 percent to 18 percent	48
Grand total	*1609*

Past experience indicates that challenges are likely in the courts on both the national and local levels as the new amendments are implemented. And implementation of new regulations will, as always, be complicated and in the early stages will be accompanied by some errors of omission or commission. I have described earlier some of the unfortunate effects of a number of court decisions. One may hope that the courts will be made aware of the administrative impact and the potentially poor cost-benefit ratios of some decisions adverse to the government. Further, it might well be that the government side, especially in situations where the administrative impact is anticipated to be severe, should, instead of accepting a consent decree, appeal the adverse decision issued by the lower court. At the very least, one might hope that the courts would restrict the remedies for administrative or regulatory defects to the future and avoid retroactive benefits when the number of households involved is likely to be relatively small and the retroactive benefits an insignificant addition to benefits already received. In sum, the courts should recognize that the food stamp program cannot be administered to guarantee perfect justice for every individual every month.

CHAPTER 5

Where Do We Go from Here?

In the preceding chapters, I have reviewed developments during much of the last two decades in public assistance, child support, and food stamps. I have underlined what I perceive as a disdain for program integrity, a reluctance to enforce family responsibility, and a rejection of the obligation to work on the part of the welfare community, many welfare officials, most black political leaders, and, to a considerable extent, the liberal white community and the courts. The intentions of Congress and state legislatures in enacting social welfare programs in pursuit of humanitarian goals have frequently been substantially modified, if not perverted, through regulation, management, and judicial decisions—and always under the banner of helping the poor and vulnerable. If this disdain, reluctance, and rejection had led to prospects for a better life for the people the programs were designed to serve, the results might have provided moral, if not political, justification. But has this been the case? The evidence is to the contrary.

The most quoted sentence in the Kerner Report, which racked the country when it was issued in 1968, was: "Our nation is moving toward two societies, one black, one white—separate and unequal."[1] More than a decade later, one can write with accuracy that the black and Hispanic communities are moving toward two societies: one composed of intact families, the other of female-headed families—separate and unequal. As early as 1970, Dr. Andrew Brimmer, then a member of the Board of Governors of the Federal Reserve System, called attention in an address at Tuskegee Institute to the "significant economic progress" made by blacks during the 1960s. He added, however, that the overall improvement hid a deepening schism in the black community, one that was evident "above all in the dramatic deterioration in the position of Negro families headed by a female." And as Dr. Robert Hill pointed out more recently, the entire rise in the number of poor black families in the seventies was accounted for by the increase in number of families headed by women. We are indeed in danger of creating a permanent underclass in the country—an un-American idea if ever there was one.

The guarantee of equal opportunity for all is widely, if not universally, supported, and much has been accomplished during the last two decades, especially through enlarging educational opportunities to give some solid backing to this guarantee. Equal outcomes, or equality of income, has never been an American goal. Nevertheless, there has been and will continue to be legitimate public debate on the issue of how much redistribution of income a society should undertake to reduce the inequality of income produced by the marketplace or the vicissitudes of life—death or ill health, divorce or desertion. The answer will change over time—in fact, it has changed over past decades—as the public perception changes with respect to the level of inequality which is acceptable or unacceptable. But surely, in a democratic system, decisions on the use of public funds should be made only by elected officials influenced by a broad consensus of public opinion. When legislative decisions are manipulated or legislative intent is ignored to achieve the ideological ends of particular groups, the public has a right to complain and to react. It did just that in the 1980 national election. But the debate will continue, as it should, on how best to reduce poverty and dependency and how best to serve those who, for a short or long period, need society's help.

One cannot look to further substantial increases in the welfare standard to solve the problems of poverty and its consequences, even assuming the return of Democrats to the President's office and the majority control of the Congress in 1984. (One may, however, hope for some increase in the welfare grants in states in the South.) Increases will come, mainly to offset the effects of inflation, but these will be minor in relation to the current total welfare package and will have little impact, if any, on the widespread social pathology evident among AFDC families.*

Nor can one look to welfare reform along the lines of Nixon's Family Assistance Plan of 1969–1971 or the Carter Program for Better Jobs and Income of 1977–1979. Both failed because, in the end, it was found that if one insisted on the humanitarian goal of a reasonable welfare grant for those who cannot work *and* a financial incentive to work for those who were employable, such a large proportion of the population became eligible for some supplementation and the cost became so enormous as to be politically unacceptable. In the case of the Carter program, the added cost was estimated at $20 billion per year, or almost twice as much as was then being spent for the AFDC program. President Carter's irritation with the financial realities of welfare reform, including adequate benefits and incentives, is dramatically described by Joseph Califano in *Governing America*, his account of his experiences as Secretary of Health, Education, and Welfare. The fate of the earlier Nixon plan is even more dramatically described by Daniel Patrick Moynihan in *The Politics of a Guaranteed Income.*

*The 15 percent increase in the basic allowance passed in the 1981 legislative session in Albany and approved by the governor will add 2.5 to 5 percent to the value of the total welfare package, depending on whether the food stamp allotment is reduced or not.

Furthermore, large-scale experiments such as the Seattle-Denver Income Maintenance Experiment, which have tested the impact of a guaranteed income with financial incentives, have shown that the result is some diminution of work effort, as well as some increase in family break-up.* As Martin Anderson has put it, "For better or worse, high marginal tax rates are an enduring part of our welfare system."[2]

We must have a welfare program, and it must provide adequate assistance. The basic humanitarianism of American society, with its profound concern for helping those in need, requires it. We do need a safety net, not only for the aged, disabled, and unemployed, but for those who cannot work because of family responsibilities or because, despite their best efforts, they cannot earn enough to provide an acceptable level of living for the family.**

We are in a period of low productivity gains and a less rapidly expanding economy. The result, as Moses Abramovitz put it in his presidential address to the American Economic Association, is that "in the now less favorable growth environment, the tensions between productivity and other welfare goals are screwed several notches tighter."[3] The level of political tension can be contained only if we can maintain program integrity and reduce dependency. The first is a short-run issue; the second is the more difficult, long-term problem.

---

*Since the results of the Seattle-Denver experiment were published, a new industry may be said to have sprung up to disprove them. The best I can make of the results is that, to the extent that the reduction of work effort was not as large as it appeared from the data, the discrepancy was matched by an increase in nonreporting of wages by those in the experimental group.

**It must be stressed that even when ineligibility and overpayments were at their height—a 27 percent payment-error rate in New York City in 1973—73 percent of the funds were properly spent. In 1980, the caseload had been reduced by about 125,000 persons and the payment-error rate was 9.7 percent; 90.3 percent was spent appropriately. The record in the food stamp program is, however, not as good.

CAN WE ACHIEVE PROGRAM INTEGRITY?

Program integrity is not a problem limited solely to the welfare system or other benefit programs such as unemployment insurance or social security. It is also of major concern in relation to the payment of individual and business income taxes, military expenditures, farm subsidies, and, in effect, to any program which involves large sums of government expenditures or tax payments. A recent article in *Barrons,* which can hardly be accused of being a radical publication, reports estimates that 15 to 25 percent of the gross national product, excluding gambling, prostitution, and narcotics, is not reported for income tax purposes.[4] The article points out that the Internal Revenue Service believes it can only begin to deal with this gross underpayment of taxes as it develops more and more sophisticated computer systems to detect fraud and abuse.

We cannot just sigh and sorrowfully agree that nothing which is useful and necessary can be accomplished without a considerable degree of fraud and abuse. The costs are enormous, and the sense of injustice among those who bear the largest part of the tax burden—that is, the middle class—becomes too acute for political comfort. Efforts must be made to reduce waste wherever it occurs.

And so it is with the public assistance program or food stamps. For too many years, too many leaders of the social welfare community claimed the welfare program was unmanageable; they, as well as many political leaders in Congress and welfare administrators at all levels of government, were relatively unconcerned with fraud and abuse. The programs are complex because the problems they deal with are complex, but they are manageable. They can be administered with reasonable efficiency and effectiveness, as efforts described in the preceding chapters have shown.

A major gap in the congeries of efforts to improve program integrity has been filled with the passage of the 1981 amendments to the Social Security Act, permitting states to establish workfare programs for AFDC mothers.* Whether and to what extent the states will take advantage of this provision remains to be seen. One can anticipate that in New York, and probably some other states as well, vigorous opposition to state and local action will be mounted by the welfare community and minority leaders. One may hope that responsible elected and appointed officials will recognize two things. First, there is much public work that needs to be done, especially in the poorer communities, and much to be gained by the welfare client from the discipline of work and the experience which is gained. Second, the offer of workfare jobs improves program integrity; experience indicates that for every 100 welfare clients offered such jobs, about ten will refuse them and accept permanent closure of the case. Only if the workfare programs are established on a large scale in relation to the size of the caseload, however, will they be effective. Otherwise, even with a high refusal rate, the available job openings are quickly filled and the work test can no longer be applied except as turnover occurs. It must be recognized, though, that initiation of large-scale workfare programs will be seriously hampered by the omission from the 1981 amendments of any federal financial contribution to the substantial cost of supplies, equipment, and supervision for the workfare projects.

Apart from workfare, the chimera of financial incentives has been replaced in the 1981 amendments by an obligation to work at available jobs, assuming these are offered at prevailing wages (which might for some jobs be the minimum wage) and under the usual safeguards which apply to business and service establishments. Admittedly, for some women, as for some male heads of families, with more than one or two children, the wages earned, even with the disregard of work expenses, may not come to as much as the welfare standard. In this connection, it may

---

*For the many welfare clients with only one child, the work would be only part-time, but for larger families it could come to be full-time. It would be more equitable to set a maximum of 20 to 25 hours per week for workfare programs.

be noted that a recent report by the U.S. Department of Labor indicated that the vast majority of job growth in recent decades has occurred in generally low-paying businesses and industries and that new jobs in the 1980s will predominantly employ secretaries and stenographers, retail sales workers, building custodians, cashiers and bookkeepers—jobs which pay about half the wage of factory jobs which are disappearing.[5] Such a trend will not necessarily mean that wages will be inadequate for family needs, but in situations where such is the case, welfare grants can be used to supplement wages. Of course, to the extent that supplementation is necessary, the number of persons on welfare will not change, but the total costs can drop dramatically.

The effectiveness of the work requirement will obviously be greatly enhanced if the general level of unemployment is substantially lower than during the last months of 1981 when it was 7 to 9 percent nationally, 8 to 10 percent in New York City, and higher in many other cities throughout the country. One may hope that supply-side economics, which Senate majority leader Howard Baker has called a "riverboat gamble," will achieve the success within a few years that its advocates anticipate. But, in the meantime, it makes no economic or social sense that the public employment aspect of CETA has been eliminated in accordance with the Reagan administration's proposal.

It is true that during the first years of the program, many state and local governments, and none more than New York City, misused CETA as a means for retaining public employees who would otherwise have been laid off because of budget cuts. But during 1979–1980 this situation was corrected, partly because of revised federal regulations, and to a considerable extent the jobs were given to welfare recipients or other disadvantaged workers for periods of specified duration. Admittedly, not as many CETA employees have moved into unsubsidized private employment as had been assumed. But in comparing the costs, which are large, to the benefits, which have been limited with regard to transition to private employment, one must not ignore CETA's effectiveness in improving the integrity of the public assistance program by providing a work test. As I indicated earlier, the offer of a CETA job to 100 welfare recipients uncovered thirty-five to forty who apparently had other sources of income, not found through computer matches or other techniques. Their refusal of the job offer permitted closure of the welfare case, and half remained closed for at least six months.

Program integrity will suffer to some degree as a result of the elimination of the CETA employment program. Only partial recompense will be obtained from workfare, since the refusal rate is lower for part-time than for full-time jobs and since, as indicated, a large-scale expansion of such programs is unlikely without a federal contribution. If only for reasons of program integrity, Congress should consider re-establishing the CETA employment program. There are, however, other good reasons for doing so. Among them: useful and necessary work is accomplished, a ladder is provided for those who start in workfare jobs and can be encouraged by the prospect of full-time employment at regular pay, and some do move into regular employment in private or public jobs because of the CETA experience.

Another matter of concern must be noted. The budget-reconciliation process was so massive and so rapid that little, if any, consideration was given to the impact of the different eligibility requirements and the caps on eligibility for the various programs on potential "notches" (the points at which an increase in earnings of, say, $100 will result in a diminution of benefits of more than $100 from the combination of public assistance and food stamps, and other programs). This is not a new problem; it has plagued social welfare programs for more than a decade. But although no detailed analysis has yet been undertaken, it is likely that the notch problem has been exacerbated. Congressional review of the issue in the near future is essential, since it becomes exceedingly difficult to enforce a work requirement if the welfare family is going to end up with less income than welfare provides.*

---

*One of the most severe disincentives to going off welfare is the loss of automatic eligibility for Medicaid. While the family with modest income and

Finally, mention must be made of an effort by the Reagan administration to improve program integrity which will boomerang. Newspaper reports in early September 1981 and regulations issued in the *Federal Register* of September 23 indicate that, despite much adverse comment from welfare administrators, the Department of Health and Human Services is defining personal property, other than one automobile and necessary household goods, as assets to be taken into account in applying the $1,000 asset limitation on eligibility for public assistance. In other words, anything from a color TV set to a silverplated tea service or a bicycle would be counted as an asset. This can only be regarded as macho make-believe; it is not enforceable even at the cost of an enormous administrative effort, including hiring various types of appraisers. Further, it is likely to distract welfare administrators and staff from the already heavy tasks involved in implementing the other 1981 amendments, which can have a beneficial impact on the integrity of the program.

Nevertheless, a significant improvement in the integrity of the public assistance program has already been achieved in New York and throughout the country. Further gains can be made with the establishment of effective work requirements, and large-scale workfare programs, especially if the missing link—a CETA

heavy medical bills may become eligible for Medicaid at a certain point, a reluctance to face the arcane complexities of "spend-down" provisions is easily understandable. This book is not the place for an extended discussion of the issue, but I must note my view that until we establish a system of national health insurance to replace the income tested Medicaid program, the incentive for remaining on welfare will be that much harder to overcome. It is worth noting a story in the *New York Times* of September 29, 1981, which dealt with the reduction in the incentive payment to AFDC mothers who are working and its limited duration. One such mother in New Jersey stated that she had no sympathy for the women who can work but who depend entirely on welfare. But she also stated that her primary concern was the loss of Medicaid benefits. One of her sons had been repeatedly hospitalized with chronic ailments. Clearly, her salary of $8,625 per year would not be adequate to cover hospital costs.

public employment program—is restored.* Amendments to the food stamp law and the regulations implementing them, which are now in place, permit a substantial reduction in ineligibility and overpayment rates in that program. These gains must be maintained and extended, a task that will require a commitment by elected and appointed officials to do so, for the gains can easily be lost if old ideologies reassert themselves in welfare policymaking or administration.

CAN WE REDUCE DEPENDENCY?

As we look to the future, we need something more than program integrity. Even if ineligibility in New York City were reduced to the tolerable level of 4 percent, I roughly estimate that as many as 750,000 to 800,000 persons would remain on welfare, excluding the aged, blind, and disabled. This is about 12 to 13 percent of the nonelderly population in the city but a much larger proportion of the city's minorities. A comparable situation is likely to hold in other cities. A future on welfare for 20 to 25 percent of a city's blacks and Hispanics is dim for them and for the cities; it is especially dim for the young in these groups.

If we are to avoid another generation or two of dependency on welfare and the social pathology that accompanies it, we must focus on three groups: the children on welfare, the young mothers fourteen to thirty years old, and the young single individuals, eighteen to thirty years of age. We must also find ways to counteract and to reverse the trend toward nonformation or break-up of families, and, above all, we must restore a sense of

---

*Theoretically, those on welfare who are working off the books and not reporting their incomes are discovered in the course of the quality control audits, which are based on extensive field investigations, and reflected in the official data on ineligibility. I suspect, however, that the field investigations are only partially successful in this regard.

family responsibility, despite the availability of the welfare "option."

As of July 1981, of the 859,000 people on welfare in New York City, 519,000 were children—498,000 of them in female-headed families. As already noted, it is these children who account for about half of the high school dropouts. They will be barred by lack of education from most of the good jobs, those paying good wages with possibilities of advancement, and if they turn to delinquency and narcotics addiction, they are likely to be barred from any kind of steady employment.

The problem is easier to describe than to solve. But surely the effort must be made, and it must start with the young children, those under twelve years of age. If a child reaches this age two years behind in reading and math, the chances of recovery and achievement of a high school diploma are slim. Further, the effort becomes very costly. Much has been tried—Head Start, federal aid to elementary schools in impoverished areas, innovative approaches introduced by different schools or school systems, special programs in remedial reading and math. Some gains have been made, and these efforts must continue. What has been lacking, however, is any significant coordinated effort by the school system and the social service side of the welfare system to work with the families—the mothers and the young children—to determine what problems are developing and what can be done to help deal with them and to provide the necessary social services to deal with problems before they turn into major crises. Indeed, while we have a large and varied public social services system in New York City, involving expenditures of more than a billion dollars per year, practically none of this money is spent in working directly with welfare families to assess their situation and to help the children achieve a successful school career.

Oddly enough, many leaders of the social work profession appear to abjure the notion that any reduction in welfare dependency can be achieved through the provision of social services, and they have even opposed efforts to demonstrate that such a plan can be successful. They take the attitude that these efforts blame the victim rather than the perpetrators, which they see as discrimination, high unemployment, bad housing, inadequate schools, and so on. In sum, their view appears to be that nothing can be done to reduce dependency until all the ills of society are corrected. Welfare administrators cannot afford such a negativistic view and should seek through a variety of demonstration programs to find the successful combination that will improve the pattern of family living and the child's chances of getting through school successfully.

Special efforts must be directed to the teenage mother with a child under three years of age to help her complete at least high school and enter the world of work. It may be hard for those outside the welfare field to believe, but it is true that for more than a decade, since the separation of social services from the provision of public assistance was mandated, local welfare agencies are not required to consider the family's social situation and determine whether and what social services may be needed. The decision whether services are needed is left to the welfare family. The concept does not make much sense for any family on welfare; it is nonsense when the welfare client is an unmarried teenager of fourteen to seventeen years who has become pregnant, or who already has a child and applies for welfare. She and her child have serious problems, whether she knows it or not, and whether or not she knows what help she may need.*

If it is difficult to deal with the problem of the young chil-

---

*A cooperative program developed early in 1981 by the Human Resources Administration and the New York City Board of Education is a good example of the type of effort required. About $285,000 of WIN funds are being used for on-site child care and social services for 150 students enrolled in special Outreach and Learning Centers as part of a program to return high school dropouts to school. It is anticipated that the provision of day care and social services will make it possible for the teenage mother who enters the program on a voluntary basis to complete high school and subsequently become employed. This is, of course, a small-scale program in relation to the size of the problem.

dren on welfare, the problems multiply with older teenagers and single men and women eighteen to thirty years old. These are the probable or actual school dropouts. (Among the eighteen- to thirty-year-olds on public assistance in New York City in 1976, 50 percent had less than a high school education.) The open college enrollment policy established in New York in 1970, and even earlier in such states as California, has provided new opportunities for education and training for every high school graduate, but these opportunities are not open to the high school dropout. Efforts to lure the dropouts back to school to obtain a diploma should continue and be expanded, but many will not respond. The dropout's prospects are probably limited to un- skilled jobs; perhaps the best course is to recognize this as a fact of life and try to move them into such jobs as quickly as possible.

The WIN program can be faulted on many grounds but on none more than its failure, indeed refusal, to target its limited resources and capabilities to those for whom the payoff is likely to be the greatest and most certain. Within the legal limits pre- viously placed on the program (only women whose children are six years old or older were required to register), it never made any sense that equal priority and attention were given to the forty-year-old woman with only a grade school education and three or four school-age children and to the woman under thirty with some high school experience or the high school graduate with only one or two children. It was almost as if there were a will to fail, or to spin wheels. The former group will indeed have great difficulty finding and keeping a job and running a household at the same time; the latter group should find it eas- ier, and day care costs would be minimal. A shift in priorities is long overdue.

The 1981 amendments now require women whose children are three or older to register for work or training and to accept employment if child care is available. Thus it becomes possible to avoid the long-term dependency which is likely to occur if one waits until the youngest child reaches the age of six. But unless efforts are focused on the younger women with only one or two children, the limited resources available to WIN are likely to be dissipated, as they have been in the past.

One of the most fascinating welfare statistics in New York, generally noted for its large magnitudes, is the *tiny* number of intact families receiving welfare. As of July 1981, 3,700 intact families were receiving assistance from the AFDC-U program and 4,150 from General Assistance, a total of 7,850, or less than 1 percent of all intact families of three or more persons in the city.* The heads of household in families receiving general assistance are usually working but not earning enough to support their larger-than-average families; thus they are receiving supplementation to bring their incomes up to the welfare standard. The heads of the AFDC-U families are either unemployed or working less than 100 hours per month; they also usually receive only supplementation of inadequate earnings or of unemployment insurance. In brief, it is uncommon for the intact family to require assistance from welfare unless unemployment reaches extraordinary heights and remains high for an extended period, as is the case, for example, in Michigan at present. Further, a study done a few years ago of cases closed for need-related reasons—such as finding a job or return of a spouse, as distinct from noncompliance with regulations—indicated that, proportionately, most such cases were intact families. In other words, intact families when they do need public assistance, need it generally only for a short time.[6]

One must conclude that the most effective way to reduce dependency is to promote the formation of intact families and prevent their break-up. A most telling comment on this issue was made in a Michigan study: "Quantitatively, the family is

---

*Some will insist that these numbers do not reflect the full extent of need among intact families. Indeed, it might be argued that until the early 1970s, complicated regulations and administrative practices prevented some significant number of needy intact families from obtaining assistance. But this has not been true for several years, especially since a 1976 court decision prohibited denial of AFDC-U benefits to families in which the head of the household was receiving unemployment insurance benefits.

still the principal income maintenance program."[7] To put it more strongly, the greatest income maintenance program which has ever been devised is the intact family. Indeed, it is only the intact family which, on average, can assure economic well-being for its members. The fact is that in the New York area, it takes on average 1.3 wage earners per four-person family to achieve the BLS lower-level standard of living of $14,393 in fall 1980 prices, 1.7 for the moderate level ($26,749), and 2.0 for the higher level ($42,763). Figures for the rest of the country are comparable. Thus the female-headed family is obviously at a disadvantage.

Data for the country as a whole indicate that in 1978, 42 percent of single-parent families headed by women had incomes below the poverty level, compared to 6 percent of two-parent families.[8] Among two-parent families with more than one earner, only 2 percent of white families and 5.5 percent of black and Hispanic families were living below the poverty level.[9] The income gap between black and white intact families has been diminishing rapidly in recent years, and among younger families it has almost disappeared.

And yet the greatest inequity in the public assistance system is that it discriminates *against* the intact family, in two ways. First, despite the availability of federal participation in funding, only twenty-six states have established AFDC-U programs to assist intact families where the father—or the mother, if she is the primary earner—is unemployed or underemployed. About the same number of states and, in the main, the same states have general assistance programs to assist intact families whose earnings from full-time employment are below the welfare standard. In the remaining twenty-four states, no assistance is offered to such families. Second, families served under general assistance programs financed by the state or locality do not benefit from the same disregards of income as AFDC families. Although these disregards have been reduced in the 1981 amendments, and although the earnings disregard of $30 and a third of net income is limited to four months, a significant sum of money is involved for low-income families. This discrimination makes no sense in a society which places great value on the family and where the intact family is the main bulwark against long-term dependency.

Both the Nixon and the Carter welfare reform proposals would have mandated assistance to intact families and provided for federal financial participation. But since both failed to pass Congress, nothing has been done to remedy the inequitable treatment of the intact family which does sometimes need financial assistance. A remedy is available, short of major welfare reform, through an extension of the AFDC-U program. First, its establishment should be mandated in all states, and, second, the restriction relating to underemployment should be removed, so that eligibility is granted to families where the head of the household is working full time but not earning as much as the welfare standard provides. The cost would not be tremendous; one estimate puts it at from $182 to $383 million per year, depending on whether the benefit level is placed at 75 percent or 100 percent of the poverty level.[10] In either event, these are small sums compared with the $13 billion devoted to the support of female-headed families. And part of this cost would only be a transfer of the fiscal burden from the states which have general assistance programs to the federal government.

Extension of the AFDC-U program would not only remove the current inequity but it might, to some degree, prevent family break-up in a period of economic stress. It must be recognized, however, that in states which have AFDC-U and general assistance programs for the intact family, family break-up and nonformation of families have nevertheless been high, and the trend continues.

Is there anything one can do to counter the trend? We are living in an era in which divorce is common among all classes of society. Families form, break up, and reform with other partners, and some family arrangements remain informal. The economic, social, and psychological consequences are not to be taken lightly even when there is enough money to go around, or at least enough to avoid the necessity for applying for welfare. But they are disastrous for those with such limited incomes that the only alternative is welfare for the women and children, even if some child support is forthcoming.

It may seem harsh, even unreasonable, to suggest that divorce or nonformation of families is acceptable (whether desirable or not) for the relatively well off but not for those with more limited income. Economic factors, however, have always been a major consideration in the decision whether to divorce or not. After all, the increase in the divorce rate accompanied not only a loosening of religious ties and traditions and changes in women's place in the labor market, but also increasing general prosperity—a prosperity which made divorce financially possible.

Some avenues are open within the welfare system for the exercise of governmental powers to counteract the trend toward family break-up and nonformation. These include more effective implementation of the child support program and more effective work requirements for women on welfare. If the support obligation is enforced, some fathers may realize the economic advantages of rejoining the family. And if the mother, now on welfare, has to work, she may find economic advantages in joining her modest income to the father's modest income, and so may the father; together they might achieve at least the BLS lower-level standard of living.

Outside of the public assistance program, we must be concerned with issues of family planning and abortion, divisive as these issues are. Moves in Congress toward removing funding for family planning centers, further restricting the use of Medicaid funds for abortions, and criminalizing abortion are ominous if the goal is a reduction in out-of-wedlock pregnancy, especially teenage pregnancy, and the consequent adverse impact on family stability and on the children. By 1979, after an increase of 50 percent in the 1970s, one out of six births in the country occurred out of wedlock. The rates were far higher for births to teenagers; about 29 percent of births to whites and 83 percent of births to blacks occurred outside of marriage, and the numbers continue to rise. In New York City, more than a third of the babies born in 1980 and 75 percent of those born to teenagers were born to unwed mothers. The problem is one of enormous proportions, despite the fact that just over half of teenage pregnancies result in miscarriages or abortion (mainly the latter).

No objection need be made to trying exhortation for chastity, as recently proposed by one U.S. senator; it is possible to imagine that exhortation if accompanied by information on the economic and social impact of teenage pregnancy might have some impact. It would be the height of folly, however, and would reflect a disregard for the welfare of children, not to have a fallback position. The recognition by Congress that exhortation was not enough, reflected in its approval of $30 million for the Adolescent Family Life Act, is a welcome step.* But one must also recognize that the sum approved bears little relation to the size of the problem and that the program is far too limited in scope. The widespread availability of birth control information and devices, and the right and the financial assistance, if necessary, to have an abortion, are essential, if we are to hope for a reversal in the trend toward increasing numbers of female-headed families.

What is needed above all, however, is a change in attitude, an increasing sense of responsibility among parents for the care of their children.** How to achieve this change in attitude? This

---

*This law is designed to provide in equal amounts for (1) health care, nutrition services, and counseling to pregnant teenagers; (2) preventive care, including maternity homes; and (3) scientific research into the societal causes and consequences of premarital sexual relations and pregnancy.

** An extreme example of the need for such a change comes from a story by Frances Clines entitled "Children of Desire," in the *New York Times Magazine* of September 30, 1979. It tells of Jeanette, aged thirteen, and Victor, aged twelve, who "combined in a twist of innocence and passion that the young mother says she will always hold dear." At the time of the story she was not quite sixteen years old and had a one-year-old baby. According to her account, "the next great step toward independence in her life will come when she is 18"—that is, when she could become a separate welfare case and obtain her own check. The story reported that Jeanette's fifteen-year-old sister was also pregnant, and that the twelve-year-old was looking forward to following the same route. Jeanette's mother was quite complacent about the family sitis where everybody throws up his or her hands, including the 1980 White House Conference on Families and Children. President Carter began, as did Johnson and Nixon before him, with the notion of strengthening the intact family; but an HEW Family Impact Task Force urged a more "neutral" model as the liberal goal. In his perceptive book, *The Futility of Family Policy,* Gilbert Steiner points out that Carter never came to grips with the difference between "the family" and "the diversity of families" as norms for a program.[11] As a result, the White House Conference degenerated into a conference on any and all types of families rather than on the intact family. Indeed, the intact family got rather short shrift in the proceedings, and little consideration, if any, was given to possible programs for the prevention of family break-up or the nonformation of families.

Steiner suggests that the prevention of dysfunction is "still beyond public policy," meaning that despite all the research which has been done, we are unable to identify in advance and know how to prevent family break-up. Currently it can be dealt with only after the fact, and even then only imperfectly. But we simply cannot let it go at that. If there is any issue related to dependency which requires solutions, partial though they may be, it is the prevention of family instability.

During the seventies the total number of American families rose by 12 percent, while those headed by women increased by 51 percent and those including a husband and wife, by only 6.6 percent. The increase in families headed by women as a result of divorce, desertion, or nonformation of a family is found among all income and all ethnic groups. It is only a simple statement of fact, however, to note that the problem is more acute among black families; at the end of the decade, two-parent families still made up 82.5 percent of all families, compared with 14.6 percent headed by a female and 2.9 percent headed by a male only. The proportion of families headed by a woman,

uation. Nowhere in this sentimentalized story of teenage pregnancy was there any indication that it was an unmitigated disaster in terms of its economic and social consequences for the teenagers and, especially, for their children.

however, varied widely by ethnic group: 12 percent among whites, 20 percent among Hispanics, and 41 percent among blacks. The economic and social disadvantages of the female-headed family, already described, are heavy.

We need a new agenda addressed to the task of finding ways to counteract trends toward family instability, ways of promoting the formation of intact families and not rest simply on repeating the past pattern of providing more public assistance and more social services to shore up female-headed families. The complexity of the problem and the range of issues which need to be considered are not to be underestimated. As illustrations, I note the following possibilities for study.

1. The opening sentence of *Anna Karenina*, Tolstoy's tale of marital discord and its consequences, is "Happy families are all alike; every unhappy family is unhappy in its own way." This is a great literary statement, and a much-quoted one. But is it true? Are all families afflicted with discord, and therefore unhappy, different from each other, or are there groupings and patterns with similar origins to the unhappiness? Can we learn something from studying how families are formed and why they break up? For example, to what extent is it the woman's decision to conceive a child out of wedlock in the hope that the pregnancy will lead to marriage? (This has not been unknown in the past, and it has often worked.) Or to what extent is it the man who wants to father a child even though he is unwilling to support the child? In this connection, account must be taken of the widespread availability of birth control information and, in states such as New York, of the ease of obtaining an abortion. Clearly, maintaining a relationship between a male and female without its resulting in the birth of a child is an option. Are there differences by education, income, age, ethnic or religious group, or degree of urbanization? Is it likely that the knowledge gained from such studies will provide a basis for useful intervention?

2. One of the demographic facts of life is that more male babies are conceived and born than female. Neonatal, infant, and child mortality rates are higher for males than for females,

long before differential activities, whether of play or employment, would explain the phenomenon. This unfortunate ratio continues through adolescence, so that at about age twenty the number of females exceeds the number of males. Is it possible that this situation creates some sense of irresponsibility among males, that since they are scarcer, they feel they have more options? There has been little medical research in the United States to determine whether steps could be taken to reduce male mortality rates, especially in the early years.* Nor have we looked at the experience of other countries, such as Sweden, which appear to have a more equal male-female ratio.

3. Little research has been done on the absent father. Again, we know that a disproportionate percentage of the absent fathers is black or Hispanic, but a significant percentage is white. What are the common characteristics of the abandoning males? Why do they refuse to assume responsibility for the support of their children? What are these absent fathers doing in terms of jobs, relationships with other women, or remarriage, and what, if any, differences prevail by income, education, age, or ethnic group?

4. How do changes in cultural attitudes come about? What can we learn from the changes which have occurred in the post–World War II period that will lead us to some understanding of what actions government or society at large can take to discourage the "bad" changes and promote the "good"? As a specific example, how can attitudes be changed so that it will be less acceptable among low-income groups for fourteen- or fifteen-year-olds to bear children out of wedlock—understanding that this is not a problem of morality, but of economic and social well-being?

*One medical scientist, Dr. Estelle R. Ramey, stated that there was "shockingly little" research on biological differences between men and women that might help both sexes lead longer and better lives. In particular, she noted that studies to enlist some of the biochemical advantages of women to aid men have not been popular among research subjects despite the clear need. *New York Times,* January 7, 1982.

No one person, or ethnic group, or intellectual discipline can develop the agenda, for the answers lie in the whole range of the social, physical, and biomedical sciences. It will take a wide spectrum of professional and ethnic groups to do it, and someone must take the lead in bringing the various groups together. Here both government and the philanthropic foundations can play a role in overcoming the prevailing reluctance to deal with the issue by providing the impetus and the funding for groups of knowledgeable persons from various professional disciplines to begin to think about what to study, and how to study it, and then to go on from there.

HAVE THE POLITICS OF WELFARE CHANGED?

Will the politics of welfare permit the action necessary to maintain and improve program integrity, reduce dependency, and provide adequate and compassionate assistance to those in need? One can anticipate the continuation of past attitudes from the welfare and food stamp advocacy groups, most of the social welfare community, and probably many minority leaders. Excessive rhetoric continues in defense of long-held positions. The Welfare Increase Coalition, representing a wide spectrum of social agencies and advocacy groups in New York City, recently circulated a pamphlet stating that the New York welfare standard was 100 percent below the survival level! A spokesperson for the Community Nutrition Services announced, "The undeniable fact is that the Reagan Administration is asking Congress to impose malnutrition on the poor, the elderly and school children as a way to achieve its budget objective."[12] And we continue to hear references to workfare as "slave labor" and objections to requiring welfare clients to take "menial" jobs. One can also anticipate attacks on welfare and social services from the special interest groups on the right, who will urge cuts in programs without policy justification just to save on expenditures and who will continue to urge an end to funding at the state and federal levels for family planning, abortion, and other services.

Is a more constructive discussion possible in place of vociferous reiteration of entrenched positions and either vehement protests against any cuts in existing social programs or strident demands for further cuts across the board without reference to needs? In my view, there is some basis for hope. A broader consensus than previously existed appears to have developed, one that recognizes the need for some pulling back on social programs and for making them more effective, not only in terms of eligibility but in terms of promoting financial independence. The general climate is changing. The Reagan administration will obviously give high priority to ensuring program integrity, and recent statements during 1981 from the Democratic leadership in the House indicate their support for this goal as well.

Change can also be found among current administrators of welfare programs, as evidenced by the statements quoted earlier from the American Public Welfare Association, stressing that welfare should not be regarded as an alternative to work but as a backup for those who temporarily cannot work. And new voices are being heard in the black community. William Raspberry, himself a black, writing in the June 30, 1980, issue of the *Washington Post*, describes a conversation with a black lawyer who says of welfare: "If you can't find a job, we'll help you find one—even make one, if necessary. But if you don't want to work, that's it. No more welfare." Raspberry adds: "You'd never know to listen to the leaders of the major civil rights groups and the anti-poverty advocates but my lawyer friend's view is very close to that of the black American mainstream."

The civil rights movement, efforts to eliminate discrimination in employment, expansion of social programs, and control of local community organizations have engaged the attention of black and Hispanic leaders for the last two decades. The effort accomplished much that was essential for progress. But the promise is unfulfilled and will remain unfulfilled until minority leaders shift their attention to ways of disengaging a significant proportion of blacks and Hispanics from reliance solely on the welfare system and to remedying the structure of the low-income minority families. Such a shift is beginning.[13]

Much will also depend on what happens at the state and local levels and how governors, mayors, state legislators, and the courts perceive the balance of forces and how they respond to pressures from the contending groups. Of special importance will be the role of the courts in the implementation of the 1981 legislation and their attitudes toward the enforcement of the child support program.

There is a danger that we will overshoot the *via media* and land on the other side, but still the wrong side, of the road. The Reagan administration is proposing further substantial cuts in social programs. The reconciliation process used to arrive at the budget for fiscal 1982 may have been necessary to break the pattern of bending to special pleaders, but the additional proposed cuts need to be examined with due deliberation in the framework of social policy goals and priorities. Only in this way can we avoid placing unfair burdens on the poor and vulnerable. The notion of block grants, at a reduced level of federal funding, needs full public discussion and careful consideration by Congress.

Wisdom does not reside solely at the state or local level, nor are the politics of welfare in states and cities less full of whirlpools of special interests. In the continuing clash between special interests and the public interest, a reasonably wide consensus must be achieved to maintain program integrity, reduce dependency, and provide adequate and compassionate help to those who will remain in need. It will take all the will and wisdom available at all levels and all branches of government and an informed and articulate expression of opinion from all sectors of the society to get there.

A Case Study in the Politics of Welfare*

AN EFFORT TO IMPROVE WELFARE HOUSING—AND WHAT HAPPENED TO IT

About $530 million a year is spent to house families and individuals on welfare in New York City, approximately 40 percent of the $1.3 billion of federal, state, and city funds currently devoted to public assistance—a program that served 873,600 persons or 341,900 cases in October 1979. Despite the expenditure of this large sum, no one is satisfied with the housing welfare clients obtain—not the welfare clients, not the welfare administrators, not the welfare or housing advocates.

Recent data on the quality of occupied housing in New York City indicate a far higher proportion of welfare clients live in dilapidated or deteriorated housing than do families not on welfare, although average rents paid by welfare clients are as much as those paid by non-welfare families at the lower end of the income scale.[1] At the same time, landlords are aggrieved at the loss of income from nonpayment

*Originally published as "An Effort to Improve Welfare Housing—and What Happened to It," in *City Almanac* 14, no. 3 (New York City: Center for New York City Affairs, New School for Social Research, October 1979): 1–15.

of rent by welfare clients and by cash flow difficulties resulting from delayed payments.

It is necessary to point out that under New York State regulations, the welfare grant includes a specific amount for rent as paid up to certain maximum limits related to the size of the family; for example, in New York City the maximum for a family of four is $218 per month. These ceilings have not been changed since they were established in 1975. Nevertheless, data from the Housing Vacancy Survey for 1978 indicate that the maximum then was $6 above the median monthly rent paid for all four-room apartments in the city and only $10 below the median for five-room apartments.[2] The possibility of improving the housing of welfare clients by substantially raising the maximum appears to be excluded both by comparison with the rents paid by relatively low-income nonwelfare families and by the financial cost such an increase would impose on state and city budgets.

At the same time, the basic allowance for food and other items in the family budget has not been changed since 1974 (and then was based on 1972 prices); even with the substantial increase that has taken place in the value of the food stamp bonus, the combined sum has not kept up with inflation. Nevertheless, in the spring of 1979, the basic allowance plus food stamps equaled 85 percent of the U.S. Bureau of Labor Statistics lower-level budget for New York City for the items covered. Also, it may be noted that workers' spendable earnings, that is, earnings net of income and social security taxes, have also been eroded by inflation since 1972.[3]

It is tempting for the welfare client to use the money granted for rent for other items—more food or clothing or other purchases. Indeed, between 1974 and 1976 welfare clients to an increasing extent were doing just that, sometimes catching up on the rent late in the month but frequently not paying rent at all for several months and then moving if they were not evicted first. The sole tool available to the New York City Human Resources Administration (HRA) to assure rent payment is that in the event of nonpayment of rent, that is, "mismanagement of welfare grant," it could place a client on a two-party check for that part of the welfare grant earmarked for rent, that is, a check made out to the client and the landlord and cashable only when signed by both, or on direct vendor payment, that is, a check made out solely to the landlord.

In 1975, as many as 26 percent of clients receiving Aid to Families with Dependent Children (AFDC) were on two-party checks mainly for rent. Federal law and regulations, however, limited such checks to 10 percent of the AFDC families receiving unrestricted grants. Thus, the city was in danger of sustaining enormous federal penalties in the shape of nonpayment of the federal share of assistance payments for the period in question. As a result, in 1976 HRA instituted special efforts to reduce the proportion below 10 percent. Building owners perforce became the household finance bankers for those welfare clients who did not pay their rents in timely fashion or at all and who could not be accommodated within the 10 percent ceiling. In 1977, accrued unpaid rent totaled over $17.6 million in 66,220 instances known to HRA when landlords complained of nonpayment.

An analysis by the New York State Welfare Inspector General's office in September 1977 revealed that 62 percent of welfare tenants who had earlier been removed from two-party check status were in arrears on rent; half owed rent for an average of 2.3 months ($391 per tenant) and half had moved owing an average of 3.2 months ($789). A report on welfare housing prepared by the Region II Federal Regional Council (which includes representatives of the Departments of Health, Education, and Welfare and Housing and Urban Development) in November 1978 indicated that more than 60,000 welfare clients had moved at least twice in the year ending June 1977, and among these approximately 37,500 were in rent arrears. Further, as of August 1977, as many as 94 percent of welfare tenants who moved were not under two-party checks. A study by the New York Urban Coalition found that at least 15 percent of all welfare families are always more than two months behind in their rent. An audit by New York City Comptroller Harrison Goldin's office of a random sampling of buildings operated by the Division of Real Property, indicated that 80 percent of welfare clients were in rent arrears. Further, according to Judge Benjamin Nolan, presiding judge of the Bronx Housing Court, 90 percent of the actions brought by landlords against tenants for nonpayment of rent in that court involve public assistance clients.

In due course, landlords rejected the banker's role by not paying property taxes. The city then took the buildings *in rem* to the extent that it is now probably the world's largest landlord at a cost in tax levy funds of $45 million in 1979, an amount that is estimated will rise substantially in 1980.

In 1977, Congress amended the Social Security Act to raise the ceiling on the use of two-party checks from 10 percent to 20 percent of the AFDC caseload. Congress also "forgave" past sins so that no penalties were imposed on New York State. Beginning in the spring of 1978, HRA began to utilize the higher 20 percent ceiling; the proportion of AFDC clients on two-party checks rose from 10 percent to 18.7 percent in September 1979. As a result, in 1979 the instances of non-payment of rent declined to an annual rate of 56,000, involving accrued unpaid rent of $14 million—a decline but still a substantial figure. In September 1979, about 36,300 AFDC cases were on two-party checks for rent payments of $7.7 million per month.

The increased use of the two-party check does not, however, help improve housing for welfare clients as much as it might. First, the system does not permit HRA to obtain assurances from landlords that they will provide necessary repairs and services within a reasonable period of time; nor can HRA prevent landlords from evicting welfare tenants for nonpayment of rent even if code violations are present in the building. Second, there is an unavoidable delay before the two-party check can be imposed.

Under current procedures, a client must mismanage his or her funds, that is, not pay rent for at least a full month, and HRA must be so informed in writing by the landlord. What with usual processing time, six to eight weeks can elapse before the client is placed on a two-party check. The client is, of course, immediately notified that HRA has instituted the restricted check and has an opportunity to indicate if there was good reason for withholding rent, such as consistent lack of heat or hot water or hazardous conditions in the building. In this event, the client is advised of how and where to seek remedies through housing code enforcement agencies. If these remedies are not obtained, HRA can help the client to move, or if the client does not move for some reason, HRA will hold the rent payment in special accounts until the landlord makes the necessary repairs. In other types of disputes between the client and the landlord (for example, the client says the rent was paid), the client can request a conference with an income maintenance center worker to resolve the issue. If it is not resolved, the client can obtain a fair hearing under the state's fair hearing procedures; in the meantime, the landlord does not get the rent money.

Concern about the problem has led various individuals and groups to consider how the "leverage" of a half billion dollars could be used to improve housing for welfare clients. Most of these proposals, however, have been on the grandiose side and would require substantial additional public funding. But such funding is not on the horizon, and so little has come out of the discussion of the issue in the last five years. Thomas Appleby, administrator of New York Region II Office of the Department of Housing and Urban Development (HUD) in a recent article said, "Each solution addresses only part of the problem" and added, "There are no magic panaceas." He listed a number of current approaches that offer some hope for improvement among them, the expansion of the system of two-party checks "so long as their issuance is tied to an agreement by the landlords to maintain and upgrade their properties."[4]

In this article, I shall tell the tale of a joint effort by HRA and the city's Department of Housing Preservation and Development (HPD) to improve housing for welfare clients—and the sad fate that befell this effort. Implementation of the proposal would not have required large-scale additional public funding inasmuch as it was based on expanded use of the two-party check for welfare clients' rent in exchange for landlords' agreements to maintain and improve their properties.

One may ask why the tale should be told. My response is that the story reflects an important aspect of the politics of welfare—and the politics do not always work for the good of the public or the welfare client. If change is to be effected, the public needs to understand how policy is made and interpreted within the complex interrelationships among federal, state, and city officials—appointed and elected— civic organizations, welfare advocates, and ethnic and other special interest groups.

The Development of the Proposal: March–August 1978

To begin at the beginning, early in 1978, I, in my position as commissioner of HRA, and Nathan Leventhal, commissioner of HPD, met, at their request, with Assemblyman Oliver Koppell of the 84th District in the West Bronx, then Bronx Borough President Robert Abrams, and a group of their colleagues who expressed their grave concern about Community Planning Districts (CPDs) 5 and 7 in the Bronx (an area roughly bounded on the south by the Cross Bronx Expressway, the north by Gunhill Road, the west by the Harlem River, and the east by Webster Avenue). They believed these areas were in danger of becoming as devastated as the South Bronx unless something was done to stem and to reverse the tide of abandonment of buildings already significant in CPD 5 and beginning in CPD 7.

They attributed much of the problem to the presence of substantial numbers of welfare clients in the areas, a significant proportion of whom were not paying their rent in timely fashion or not paying at all and moving out when threatened with eviction. Cash flow was a serious problem for landlords in the areas as was, of course, profitability. These Bronx officials, as well as Commissioner Leventhal and I, were well aware of the many and complex causes of housing deterioration in New York City and other urban areas, but clearly nonpayment or delayed payment of rent by welfare clients was one important factor.

We explained the constraints of federal and state regulations and specifically that we anticipated we would soon be pressing against the 20 percent ceiling in view of the increasing requests from landlords throughout the city, as well as from the city itself, that tenants in *in rem* housing be placed on two-party checks. We promised, however, that we would consider the problem and try to develop something workable.

We moved quickly to hire a special consultant to develop a proposal in cooperation with HRA and HPD staff members. By early April 1978, we had agreed on the core of the plan that, for the first time in efforts to deal with this problem, was based on close cooperation between HRA and HPD.

In order to overcome the constraints of the provisions of the Social Security Act limiting the proportion of AFDC clients on two-party checks and prohibiting clients from voluntary acceptance of such checks in the absence of mismanagement of the welfare grant, it was decided to develop the project on a demonstration basis under Section 1115 of the Social Security Act. This method permitted us to request a waiver of the relevant provision of the law. It also meant, however, that implementation of the proposal required the approval of the New York State Department of Social Services (NYSDSS), which had to submit it to the U.S. Department of Health, Education, and Welfare (HEW), as well as the approval of HEW. Further, as a result of a court-induced agreement entered into by HEW in 1972 in connection with a New York State proposal for a demonstration project relating to public service employment of welfare recipients, the New York City-based Center on Social Welfare Policy and Law, as the surrogate for the defunct

National Welfare Rights Organization, would have thirty days to review and comment on the proposal. The route, as will become evident, was strewn with obstacles.

Elements of the Proposal The proposal, at this stage, included the following major elements:

Landlords in CPDs 5 and 7 in the Bronx would be encouraged to make agreements with HPD-HRA to undertake necessary repairs using Maximum Base Rent (MBR) standards (removal of rent impairing violations and 80 percent of all other violations) in accordance with an agreed-upon schedule, and to maintain their buildings and provide basic services such as heat and hot water.

In exchange, HRA would identify welfare tenants in the buildings and place them on two-party checks for rent—whether or not they had mismanaged their funds in the past.

Welfare clients in the area would be informed of the demonstration and its purposes and advised that those who were paying their rent regularly had the right to "opt out" of the two-party check requirement, that is, to refuse to participate in the project.

HPD-HRA would establish a site office located centrally in the demonstration area and staffed by HRA and HPD to (1) inspect project-enrolled buildings regularly to assure continued adequate maintenance; (2) monitor buildings that needed to be brought up to MBR standards; and (3) investigate tenant complaints that landlords were not adhering to the agreements.

If a landlord failed to adhere to the agreement for repairs or adequate maintenance, HRA would terminate the two-party check arrangement and assist the tenant to relocate.

A research component would evaluate the results of the demonstration.

The proposal was designed to test the hypothesis that prompt and regular payment of rent by welfare clients would permit landlords to begin necessary repairs and provide required building maintenance and services and would thus provide better housing for welfare clients and ultimately result in stabilizing the neighborhood housing environment. I should add that the demonstration was to be limited to buildings in which welfare clients constituted 20 percent or more of all tenants; thus, prompt payment and avoidance of arrears could make a difference in the landlords' cash flow and profitability and help assure sufficient funds for repair and maintenance.*

According to our data, 2,035 inhabited buildings were in CPDs 5 and 7. In 908 of these buildings, welfare clients comprised 20 percent or more of all tenants, with somewhat more than 600 of the buildings, housing 9,600 welfare clients, in CPD 5 and the remainder, with 2,400 clients, in CPD 7. We estimated that the extension of the two-party rent check would potentially assure the landlords of about $500,000 per month in addition to the rents collected from welfare clients already paying rent regularly. Since public assistance clients lived in about one-third of all occupied rental units in CPDs 5 and 7, this amount of additional cash had substantial potential for upgrading housing when tied to landlord agreements to repair and maintain their properties.

This core proposal, developed with assistance from Assemblyman Koppell, was circulated for review and comment to appropriate staff of HRA and HPD, NYSDSS, HEW's Regional Office, and two former HRA commissioners, James Dumpson and Mitchell Ginsberg. There was no disagreement with the proposal's general design—the use of the two-party check in exchange for a landlord's agreement to repair and maintain the building—but the comments received indicated a need to strengthen the requirements placed on the landlord and to provide additional protection to the client. Thus, some major modifications were made to (1) require a *signed* agreement from the landlord to maintain and/or upgrade buildings; (2) notify welfare tenants in project buildings *prior* to their being placed on two-party checks (as before, clients could "opt out" if they had no history of mismanagement); and (3) require HPD to schedule inspections every six months; additional inspections would be triggered by tenant complaints.

The "Second Draft"   By early June 1978, a "second draft" was completed and informally distributed for comments from individuals representing a wide variety of groups in the city. These included not only the agencies that had reviewed the first draft but also the Regional

---

*One critic of the proposal felt that the minimum proportion of welfare clients should have been 5 percent instead of 20 percent because even a small loss in rents can adversely affect revenues for repair and maintenance.

Office of the Department of Housing and Urban Development (HUD) and the New York State Division of Housing and Community Renewal, as well as elected officials such as Senator Daniel Patrick Moynihan and Congressmen Jonathan Bingham, Robert Garcia, and Charles Rangel; members of the State Assembly from the areas, including George Friedman, John E. Flynn, and Sean P. Walsh; State Senator Joseph Galiber; members of the City Council, including Stanley Simon, Wendell Foster, and Jerry Crispino from the Bronx areas interested in the project, and Aileen Ryan, Chairwoman of the Council's Welfare Committee; and such voluntary agencies as the New York Urban Coalition, the Protestant Welfare Social Policy Committee, United Neighborhood Houses, the Legal Aid Society, the New York City chapter of the National Association of Social Workers, and the Center on Social Welfare Policy and Law.

We did not obtain universal agreement with the general design from all these diverse groups, but then that would have been too much to anticipate with respect to such a controversial matter. It must be remembered that the issue of increasing the limit on the use of restricted checks, whether two-party or vendor checks, from the 10 percent level and permitting clients voluntarily to request such checks for payment of rent or utilities was hotly debated in Congress in 1977, and many social welfare organizations and welfare advocates opposed any changes. In the end, Congress was persuaded, mainly by state welfare administrators, such as Philip Toia from New York and John Dempsey from Michigan, that such an approach was essential to prevent further housing abandonment on a large scale; it did vote to increase the ceiling on the proportion of clients who could be placed on restricted checks from 10 percent to 20 percent, but it did not approve the provision for voluntary requests from clients to be placed on restricted checks.

Among many who did support the general design of the project, concern was again expressed that the second draft did not adequately protect the welfare clients either with respect to obtaining their *informed* consent to participation and use of the two-party check or to ensuring their rights if landlords did not adhere to the agreement for repairs and maintenance.

In revising the second draft, we took these concerns into account and developed procedures to ensure the clients' understanding of the demonstration, the nature of the commitment they would make, and the obligations of the landlords. Specifically, we promised that all welfare tenants in the enrolled buildings would, *before conversion* of the grant for rent to two-party checks, be clearly notified of the demonstration project and its intent. They would be asked to notify the project site office if they did not wish to participate in the demonstration. The recipient would be notified of the condition for "opting out," that is, an examination of HRA records to verify no mismanagement of the rent grant within the preceding six months.

On August 4, 1978, I was able to transmit to Barbara Blum, commissioner, New York State Department of Social Services, the "final" version of the proposal for submission to HEW. In my covering letter I stated:

> The proposed demonstration, which is now being formally submitted, has been shaped by the various comments that have been received and specifically addresses itself to the issues raised by your staff after their review of the first draft. The following changes have been made since the first draft was shared with the State:
>
> The recipients who live in enrolled buildings will be notified of the intent of the demonstration before two-party rent checks are instituted. They will also be informed that if they have no record of rent mismanagement in the immediate past six months, they can opt out. In instances where there has been mismanagement (in the prior six months) and the tenant says that he does not want to participate, he will, nevertheless, be placed on two-party checks and be advised of his right to fair hearing.
>
> The introduction was rethought and rewritten to present a more balanced concern for the tenant and the landlord. (Some who have reviewed the first draft felt that the material unduly emphasized the landlord's plight without forcefully stating the tenant's side of the story.)
>
> A community involvement component has been built in so that information about the project is made available to recipients, tenants, and community residents in the area *before* the demonstration begins.
>
> An emphasis was placed on HRA's mandated responsibility, payment for sound environment for the families, children, and individuals who are recipients, and the intent of the demonstration was more clearly stated as the intent to use the leverage of HRA rent payments to assure

continued housing maintenance/repair for the tenants while making it possible for the landlords, who specifically agree to continue to maintain or repair, to have assurance of regular rent payment from recipients.

The site office scope was broadened to include provision for acting as a broker (mediator) on the tenant's behalf in tenant-landlord maintenance or repair disagreements. A capacity for referral for problems other than housing is now also provided in the site office.

I believe that the above-mentioned changes are responsive to such criticism as has been made of this demonstration and should eliminate or lessen potential opposition to it. Informal discussions with HEW indicate that they find the concept of the demonstration of interest, and a discussion of the proposed demonstration with Henry Freedman [director of the Center on Social Welfare Policy and Law] leaves me cautiously optimistic, and . . . elected officials' support is not lacking.

I had anticipated, in the light of our extensive discussions with NYSDSS and HEW officials, as well as with the wide variety of groups already described, that the project would be formally submitted to HEW within a few weeks and I hoped for an affirmative decision by the end of September 1978. Mayor Koch was more prescient. In a memo to me, dated June 19, 1978, he said with respect to the project: "I would suggest that we set up a meeting with Joseph Califano [then HEW Secretary] when he next comes to town so as to fill him in because he will ultimately be importuned to oppose that matter." Indeed he was importuned, as was Governor Carey.

The proposal met with vociferous opposition and equally fervent support. In order to understand how the proposal was dealt with at the state and federal levels, it is necessary to describe and analyze the nature and content of the support and the opposition as public interest groups, as well as elected officials, actively sought to influence the decision to approve or disapprove the request for a waiver.

The Alignment of Support and Opposition

Organizations concerned with the condition of housing and civic groups with concern for the overall well-being of the city, as well as real estate groups, supported implementation of the plan; welfare advocates and social welfare organizations led the opposition.* Among public officials, most of those representing the Bronx areas, whether in the Congress, State Senate or Assembly, or City Council, supported the demonstration although a few remained uncommitted or silent.** One congressman, Charles Rangel of Harlem, opposed it, as did Carol Bellamy, president of the City Council. The city's major newspapers, *Times*, *Post*, and *News*, supported the proposal and urged that the demonstration was worth trying.

In general, the questions that divided these groups and individuals were: first, what were the principal factors responsible for the decline of the city's housing stock; second, were the limitations that the use of the two-party check would impose on welfare recipients justified; third, did the absence of legislative action to increase the basic welfare allowance justify the client's use of the rent grant for other purposes?

Those who found that one of the major causes of deteriorating housing is the difficulty of providing adequate services and maintenance in the face of increasing rent arrearages viewed the demonstration as a useful way to address the problem of landlords' negative cash flow. Duncan Elder, cochairperson of the New York Housing Conference, wrote to HEW Secretary Califano (November 30, 1978): "We are faced with a situation where public assistance recipients are concentrated in deteriorating buildings which have serious cash flow problems. One significant cause of the negative cash flow is rent arrearages

*The contradictory views of the housing advocates and the welfare advocates were sometimes evident within the same organization. Thus, the Community Service Society (CSS) in November 1978 denigrated cash flow as a cause of housing deterioration in criticizing the two-party check proposal. But in August 1979, in *Reforming the Community Development Program: The Key to Housing Rehabilitation*, the CSS said in commenting on the Community Management Program for *in rem* Housing: "*Cash flow* and the ability of rents to meet expenses in CMP buildings will be a critical factor in the evaluation of the success of the program. Because CD funds are not expected to be available to the program for an unlimited period of time, *building solvency* is imperative." This paragraph was, of course, written by a CSS committee on housing.

**State Senator Joseph Galiber supported the proposal in the summer of 1978 but, in mid-September 1979, announced that he had reversed his position.

which have been rising steadily and which are a main factor in poor building maintenance and a lack of building services." The use of two-party checks, he said, would guarantee an income stream to the landlord, thereby making the provision of essential services and building maintenance financially feasible. In a letter to Secretary Califano, dated December 21, 1978, Allan Talbot, executive director of the Citizens Housing and Planning Council, agreed: "An expanded system of two-party checks would curb the currently high rate of rent arrearages among welfare tenants."

State assemblymen representing the areas in the Bronx involved in the demonstration lent their support, stating that the loss to landlords of millions of dollars in rent had a devastating effect on the entire economy of New York City, particularly the Bronx. Assemblyman John E. Flynn, of the 35th District, wrote in an early letter to me, June 7, 1978: "I fully realize the importance of this approach to maintain a better housing environment and to keep the residents in our Bronx Community."

Although it was clear to many that the use of the restricted check would stabilize the income of landlords, there was still the issue of its impact upon welfare tenants. Negotiation of the two-party check was dependent upon the signature of both the tenant and the landlord, thereby providing the welfare recipient with enough leverage to demand adequate service delivery. The two-party check would not infringe upon the tenant's ability to withhold rent from a landlord who was not providing the necessary services. "In our opinion," wrote Duncan Elder to Secretary Califano, "upgrading the housing in which public assistance recipients live will give them the best housing for their rent dollar. Any rights that may be forfeited by their voluntary participation are negligible when compared to their right to a decent home."

It is important to remember that in no case would the program have operated where the landlord did not adhere to the repair schedule established by the HPD-HRA inspection unit, or where a tenant who had been paying the rent did not want to be placed on restricted checks. In a November 20, 1978, letter to Secretary Califano, Ernestine Freidlander, president of the Women's City Club of New York, outlined the group's support for the program and concern for the rights of welfare recipients: "In this case, tenant interests are safeguarded by the fact that this is a limited time demonstration project subject to public scrutiny. Welfare recipients will benefit from improved housing conditions and we also believe that they will find that they are better accepted by their neighbors."

Some felt that the demonstration would expand housing choices for welfare families. In his letter to Secretary Califano, Allan Talbot explained it was common practice among owners of sound buildings to rent to welfare recipients only if they were on two-party checks because rent payments were guaranteed. Thus, the program would increase rather than decrease welfare tenants' opportunities for better housing.

Supporting the project, Ruben Klein, president of the Bronx Realty Advisory Board, in a December 5, 1978, telegram to Secretary Califano said: "The issue at this point in time is not whether welfare clients will have the right to withhold rent from the landlords who fail to maintain their property . . . but whether there will be any rental housing left in the Bronx for welfare recipients to live in."

The Center on Social Welfare Policy and Law, and its subsidiary, the Downtown Welfare Advocate Center (DWAC), spearheaded the movement against implementation of the project. In a six-part comment addressed to NYSDSS Commissioner Barbara Blum, on August 21, 1978, DWAC outlined its view of the causes of housing decay; explained why the use of restricted checks would erode the "money payment principle," the right of AFDC recipients to spend their grant as they best determine; and questioned whether the pilot project was a legitimate experiment.

DWAC's position paper proposed a combination of increased welfare benefits and government subsidized rehabilitation loan programs as the way to improve housing in place of what DWAC regarded as a narrow focus on nonpayment of rent.

The DWAC paper went on to say that the use of restricted checks would hinder the ability of welfare recipients to control their income since often these tenants will use rent money to buy other essential goods or to provide the services that the landlord will not.

> Never was this point more dramatically illustrated than in recent winters in New York City, when landlords simply failed to provide heat. Many welfare recipients survived these winters only by using their rent money for individual self-help—for example, buying space heaters, additional heavy clothing, paying the cost of running ovens constantly—or for group self-help—such as when tenants put

their rent money together and arranged for boiler repairs to be made or for fuel to be provided.

Of course, DWAC failed to recognize that tenants would not have to resort to these measures if the project were implemented because the HPD-HRA monitoring unit would require the delivery of essential services.

DWAC also opposed the waiver of the 20 percent ceiling, stating that its purpose was to ensure that welfare agencies initiated the restriction only in cases of extreme mismanagement of funds. "This protection is needed because of agency susceptibility to internal and external pressures to control recipients' benefits." The center added that the waiver was not needed since only 11 percent of the city's welfare recipients are guilty of mismanagement. As previously noted, we anticipated that the ceiling would be reached and, as of September 1979, it did reach 18.7 percent.

DWAC also attacked the demonstration project as a legitimate social science endeavor: "As currently designed, the project will not provide valid and reliable conclusions about the effect of 'rent guarantees' on housing conditions."

Many other special interest groups echoed the complaints of DWAC. In a December 26, 1978, letter to Secretary Califano, Lloyd B. Silverman and Douglas J. Seidman of the Bronx Legal Services Corporation agreed that the use of two-party checks would violate the basic "money payment principle," remove the major leverage against landlords providing inadequate services, and impose considerable recipient hardship. The Community Service Society also cited these criticisms in a November 9 letter to Commissioner Blum, adding:

> Any program which hopes to succeed cannot fail to recognize the inadequacy of public assistance grants, the inability of the City to enforce its own housing code at the present time, the positive effects that tenant organizations can have on preserving housing when landlords fail to do so, the deleterious effects of bank disinvestment and the fact that some governmental policies themselves play a significant role in neighborhood deterioration.

Another organization that expressed similar reservations was the Task Force on the New York City Crisis. In a December 4, 1978, letter to Barry Van Lare, associate commissioner for HEW's Office of Family

Assistance, Sanford Solender and Bertram Beck, chairmen of the task force, viewed the project as too narrowly focused to address adequately all the causes of housing deterioration, as violating the basic rights of clients to spend their grants as they desired, and as neglecting to recognize the most grievous problem—inadequate benefit levels.[5]

Finally, the United Neighborhood Houses of New York, Inc., joined the DWAC bandwagon. In a December 8 letter to Califano opposing the project, Aileen C. Whittenstein, president, added that the administrative mechanism to ensure housing code enforcement, the HPD-HRA legal and inspection staff, was inadequate. She went on to say: "Implicit in this proposal, is the assumption that welfare recipients are in large part responsible for the deterioration of the neighborhoods."

Another group particularly interested in the impact of the project on welfare recipients was the New York City chapter of the National Association of Social Workers. The local affiliate noted in a December 8 letter to Secretary Califano that "public assistance recipients are facing a decreasing level of purchasing power—their income is fixed at 1971 levels, while inflation has increased unabated." This, according to the group, has caused many recipients to spend rent money on the more immediate needs of their families. "To impose rent restrictions, i.e., two-party rent payment, universally on all clients in a particular area, is an unjustified hardship on the clients and is not accompanied by any guarantees of improvement in housing services."

The most vocal opponents among elected officials were City Council President Bellamy and Congressman Rangel. Council President Bellamy argued in a December 14 letter to Governor Carey that the proposed project would not meet its goal of improving the quality of housing in CPDs 5 and 7, would infringe upon the legal rights of recipients, and would delay the development of more effective solutions to the problem of declining housing. She also questioned the ability of HRA and HPD to enforce the contracts outlining repair schedules: "The City is probably not capable at the present time of following up on inspections with legal sanctions against recalcitrant landlords."

In 1977, Congressman Rangel introduced the amendment that increased the proportion of recipients who could be placed on restricted checks because of mismanagement, and at an early stage in the discussions of the Bronx demonstration project he assured me in a telephone conversation that he would not oppose it. As opposition mounted, however, he issued a press release on December 22, 1978, claiming that the "increasing tendency to solve problems at the expense of the poor perpetuated a condition where the victim is again responsible for his victimization." In the press release, he also questioned the ability of the overburdened HRA to administer yet another procedure—namely, the enforcement of the agreements with the landlords. He suggested that a better answer might be to "go after" the delinquent landlords who find it more profitable to walk away from buildings or, worse, burn them.

Against the background of these dissonant choruses of support and opposition we can now turn to developments during the review of the proposal by the state Department of Social Services.

The State Considers the Proposal: September–December 1978

In early September 1978, a letter to me from Sydelle Shapiro, NYSDSS Deputy Commissioner for Income Maintenance, indicated our August 4 submission had been reviewed and that the changes "were responsive to our earlier questions and suggestions," but there were some "additional concerns which need clarification." These dealt mainly with the AFDC recipients' role. Could a voluntary participant withdraw at a later date? Will arrangements for housing inspections protect the recipients' privacy, and could they refuse an inspection? If participants wish to move, will case action to remove the two-party check requirement be timely enough to permit them to do so? The letter concluded that "since the outstanding issues are not *major ones* [italics added], it should be possible to make a timely submittal to HEW." Within the framework of previous conversations, "timely" meant in time for HRA to start the project before the 1978–1979 winter season. But as pressure mounted from opposing groups, NYSDSS raised more and more questions and the negotiations became prolonged.

At the heart of the opposition was an extreme reluctance to see the device of the two-party check broadened to ensure its use for rent payments, a reluctance that could only be overcome, if it could be at all, by dotting every *i* and crossing every *t* to protect the client against all contingencies, imagined and not yet imagined. The discussions between state and city officials were frequently tense as HRA and HPD strove to prevent the imposition of procedures that would make the project impossible to implement and of little benefit to building owners whom we had to encourage to sign agreements to make necessary repairs and maintain services. In part, we were suffering from the past ineffectiveness of building inspections and code enforcement and a lack of recognition of improved HPD performance and, in part, from the stereotyped image of the landlord as the villain.

In any event, we agreed to detailed provisions as to how the written notice to tenants would be worded, how we would handle different types of tenant responses, the timing of a second notice to those who failed to respond to the first notice, and the contents of a third notice to those who failed to respond to the second. We retained the right, however, to place on two-party checks clients who did not respond to the first and second notices whether there was a history of past mismanagement or not, in order to ensure, as much as possible, necessary cash flow for landlords.

With these changes, it appeared that we had the approval of NYSDSS and, indeed, on October 17, we were advised by Commissioner Blum's office that the proposal was being forwarded to HEW for early review. Mayor Koch, most concerned to achieve early implementation of the project, wrote to Secretary Califano on November 6 urging "immediate review and approval." The mayor noted that:

> If we can mount the project before the winter months, we might be able to assure heat and hot water for many of New York City's tenant/recipients in those buildings in which erosion of cash flow has prevented even the well intentioned landlord from cleaning and/or repairing the boiler.
>
> The City of New York as a result of abandonment by private landlords is now, or will be at the end of the year, the unhappy possessor of more than 55 thousand occupied apartments in dreadful condition requiring that we spend in this fiscal year $45 million for repair services to provide heat and hot water. We must do what we can to keep existing multiple dwellings now in private hands instead of ours and this is one way to assist that endeavor.

It turned out, however, that Commissioner Blum *did not sign* the appropriate form in submitting the proposal to HEW on October 17; therefore, it was not a formal submission. If we thought we had overcome the most formidable obstacles, we were again disappointed. In late October, we learned—for the first time—that the project could not be officially submitted without review by NYSDSS's Institutional Review Board. Second, NYSDSS had more questions; third, HEW now had its questions to raise; and fourth, the chorus of opposition, as well as support, now directed its attention to Washington.

First, we shall deal with the additional questions from NYSDSS. After a number of meetings in late October and early November 1978 (following the submission of the unsigned proposal to HEW) between state and city officials involved in the project, Commissioner Blum and I met to see whether we could agree on a final list of questions to which we would seek to provide answers. She gave me her list on November 22 and I responded on the 29. The state now wanted assurance that buildings with rent impairing violations (which endanger the health, safety, or welfare of tenants) would not be included in the demonstration until those violations were corrected, that enrolled buildings would be more frequently inspected to reduce risks of violations, and it wanted a fixed time frame for correction of different types of violations.

In response to these requests, we specified the standards for building selection. These included proper registration of buildings with appropriate agencies relating to fire prevention and rent regulations, an acceptable owner-managing agent history with HPD, an acceptable renting plan if vacancies exceeded 15 percent, no more than ten housing code violations per housing unit, no outstanding tax arrears, and no building with an unsafe designation by the Department of Buildings at the time of enrollment or subsequently. We also agreed to an increase in the frequency of regular inspections of enrolled buildings from once every six months to once every three months (although this, of course, increased costs and was not essential since we had already agreed to ad hoc inspections if there were tenant complaints). This change had a droll consequence later at the HEW level of decision. We could not, however, state in advance of project implementation, the amount of time necessary for various repairs.

The state brought up again a different type of issue, which related to clients in enrolled buildings who had not mismanaged funds during the six months prior to project implementation. The state again requested that if such clients did not respond to written notices, they not be placed on two-party checks without a face-to-face contact between the client and HPD-HRA staff. In my response of November 29, I said:

I am at a loss to understand why this issue is being raised
since at a meeting in your offices attended by [my represen-
tative] Harriet Dronska, Assemblyman Oliver Koppell, and
your Deputy, Sydelle Shapiro, agreement was reached on
client enrollment and participation. . . . Insistence on the
face-to-face contact would in effect make this project so costly
in terms of manpower effort that it would amount to your
effectively preventing this project from being implemented.

I also committed HRA legal staff to develop an informed consent notice to clients that would include an explanation of the "risks" of participating in the demonstration project.

Commissioner Blum's list also contained questions about the research and evaluation component, most of which I felt could be left to
staff. But one relating to a control group was important, and it was to
be with us to the end. We had rejected the notion of the inclusion of
a control group as unfeasible on the grounds that situational variables
in different areas would have to be identified and accounted for and
that, in effect, it was not possible to do this at a reasonable cost. In
our view, it was sufficient to establish criteria to determine on a "before and after" basis whether better housing for welfare clients resulted from the use of two-party checks in return for the landlords'
agreement to maintain their buildings.

I also rejected the notion that a preliminary study to gather base-
line data was necessary, since sufficient data were, in fact, available,
and "a preliminary study requirement can only be interpreted as an
effort to delay the project interminably." I urged that our staffs get
together quickly to resolve the remaining research issues and concluded by saying: "I think you know my sense of urgency regarding
this project. The winter is upon us and I dread to think that the intri-
cacies of institutional politics might have cost some of our clients the
comforts of heated premises."

A further exchange of letters on December 6 and 7, 1978, covering
relatively minor points, seemed to resolve all outstanding matters, and
on December 13, Commissioner Blum forwarded the redrafted proposal to Barry Van Lare at HEW. But while she pointed out the major
changes in the project, she also indicated to Associate Commissioner
Van Lare that she still had reservations. Her letter to him indicated
that NYSDSS's Institutional Review Board had not completed its review, though it had already held three meetings, and took note of

questions the review board had raised on the subject of "human risk."
She also said:

> Finally, we have serious reservations as to the degree to
> which this project will have an impact upon the housing
> problems in New York City. Therefore, to insure positive
> outcome to the degree possible, we feel we must reserve the
> right to review the final procedures developed to implement
> this project. In addition, this Department plans to work with
> other relevant agencies to help develop several additional
> projects which incorporate various approaches to New York
> City's housing problems.

Commissioner Blum did convene an interagency group of state and
city officials, which began meetings in early 1979 to consider alternative approaches. So far, no specific proposals have been developed.

In the meantime, on the assumption that the request for a waiver
would be approved so that the project could go forward, HRA and
HPD staff began the detailed work on the location of the site office,
selection of staff for this office, and preparation of forms in addition
to dealing with the myriad of details that had to be worked out with
respect to inspections and other matters to implement the demonstration. Thousands of man-hours went into this effort over the succeeding months.

The Institutional Review Board: November 1978–January 1979

We now come to the Institutional Review Board (IRB). But before
discussing its role in this particular project, it is worth reviewing briefly
the origins of this type of institution. The move to establish such boards
began about a decade ago, mainly out of concern for protecting the
rights of potential subjects for experimentation with new drugs, medical techniques, or psychiatric or psychological treatment or techniques. Certainly, no one would take exception to efforts to ensure
that the subjects of such experiments clearly understood the risks.

In the intervening years, however, the concepts of "informed
consent" and "risk" have been vastly broadened to the point where if
a survey involves, for example, interviews with welfare clients to obtain responses to questions about efforts to obtain employment or their

attitudes toward work, it becomes necessary to obtain approval from an institutional review board indicating that the clients interviewed are not subjected to undue risk. It is not altogether clear, however, when a proposed study or demonstration involves risk, and when it must be approved by such a review board.

Thus, since federal regulations permit placing welfare clients on two-party checks if they mismanage their funds, it came as a surprise to HPD-HRA officials when, many months after planning for development of the project began with the knowledge of HEW and NYSDSS officials, we were informed in late October 1978 that the NYSDSS Institutional Review Board would have to review the project to determine whether clients would be subject to undue risk.

During its first three meetings in November and December, the review board considered three issues: (1) jurisdiction of the board; (2) whether the project placed "subjects," that is, the welfare clients, at risk; and (3) if they were at risk, the degree to which the proposal met the required criteria.

With respect to jurisdiction, the board decided its jurisdiction was unclear and wrote to HEW counsel to seek clarification. With respect to whether the welfare clients would be placed at risk, the minutes of the board's meetings indicated two points of view:

> Under current practice, persons are placed on two-party checks because of mismanagement. Therefore, some IRB members argued that since this is federal, state, and local policy, this requirement alone in the proposal cannot be considered to be placing a person "at risk" as defined by HEW regulations.
>
> Other members have noted that existing policy may place a person at risk, unless implemented properly. To expand that policy to persons not mismanaging funds, and in a situation where there is no assurance that landlord compliance will occur, may place such persons at risk for several reasons. They lose their right to negotiate with the landlord for building compliance. Recipients lose the ability to utilize shelter benefits to pay for housing repairs, when the landlord does not provide such functions. Finally, recipients lose their ability to utilize limited funds to meet ongoing or emergency needs, because of the loss of about one half of their regular benefits.

On the third point, the board's discussion of whether the demonstration would succeed was summarized as follows:

There is concern that no benefits will materialize for subjects, for several reasons. First, stabilizing cash flow may not result in landlord compliance. Most recipients live in 40–50 unit apartment dwellings. Assuming 20 units are composed of public assistance recipients which receive approximately $200 per month for shelter, that will result in about $40,000 per year to the landlord in rent. In many instances, those funds will be insufficient to eliminate health and building code violations. Other funding sources, such as capital improvement loans, should be made available. Finally, deterioration of housing and neighborhoods is a function of other factors such as availability of city services (sewage, street repair, police and firemen, etc.). These issues must also be addressed if one seeks to achieve and maintain adequate housing.

It also has been noted that the ability of New York City to achieve code compliance has not been outstanding. It is unclear in the proposal whether housing inspection staff will be utilized in greater numbers than is current practice.

Concerning knowledge to be gained from the proposal, it was noted that the evaluation design and proposed staffing are weak. In particular, any specificity about measuring and evaluating client impact is missing. It also may be inappropriate for HRA to be undertaking the evaluation, least of all with no additional funding.

The review board also questioned the legality of placing clients with no history of mismanagement who do not respond to the request to participate in the project on restricted checks without their written consent. It concluded, "The board is concerned about these issues, but has not made any formal recommendations, other than to request clarification of jurisdiction from HEW."

The confusion reflected in this status report not only with respect to jurisdiction but with respect to the matters the board was undertaking to consider, if it considered the project at all, led Mayor Koch to write Robert Morgado, secretary to the governor, on December 29, 1978, requesting his intercession to obtain a decision from the review board:

Considering the great need for the project and the wide approval it has received from the legislators and community leaders in the Bronx district, as well as the editors of the *New York Times,* I find the more than three-month delay in the formal submission of the project to HEW unreasonable. In addition, the State Department of Social Services' Institutional Review Board which met three times over several weeks was unable to decide whether or not it had jurisdiction or to decide the issues which it raised.

Commissioner Bernstein spoke to Mr. Barry Van Lare, of the Department of Health, Education, and Welfare (HEW), on December 27. He feels that it is necessary for the Institutional Review Board to pass on the project. Furthermore, an agreement between HEW and the National Welfare Rights Organization stipulates that the Welfare Rights Organization has the right of review and recommendation on demonstration projects requiring HEW waivers. The Welfare Rights group will not consider our project, however, until the Institutional Review Board has approved it. We are again in a Catch 22 situation.

It seems clear that the State Department of Social Services' Institutional Review Board must take immediate action.

HEW never responded in writing to the request for clarification of the review board's jurisdiction, but Barry Van Lare orally requested Commissioner Blum to have the board consider the issue. Thus, NYSDSS convened a meeting on January 8, 1979, to reach a decision. Since we learned that representatives from the Center on Social Welfare Policy and Law were to attend this meeting, HRA and HPD requested that their representatives also be present; NYSDSS observers also attended.

At the meeting, Henry Freedman, director of the Center on Social Welfare Policy and Law, circulated a brief attacking the proposal. His main points were: (1) "The Demonstration Project has aroused tremendous opposition because of the harm it threatens," and he listed various individuals and groups who opposed it; (2) he agreed with the reported views of some members of the review board that some families not now subject to two-party checks and those who had paid their rent regularly would be subject to them and, therefore, would be at risk since they "will lose rights vis-a-vis their landlords and will be less able to cope with emergencies"; and (3) he expressed doubt the project would substantially benefit clients or meet HEW's informed-consent requirement.

Mr. Freedman also warned the board that it must make an "intensive" review and indicated the possibility of litigation challenging the project. Further, he objected to the absence of written procedures governing the review board and argued that it could only conclude that the project places "human subjects" at risk and must be disapproved as not meeting HEW regulations.

As the discussion proceeded, review board members expressed their "personal" opinions against the demonstration, some using such emotional phrases as "moral outrage." Finally, some rationality prevailed as one member pointed out that federal law and regulations permitted use of two-party checks and that in New York City, 16 percent of AFDC families were already under this restriction. Thus, participants in the demonstration would not be subjected to further risk than they were currently. The board then voted four to one that the project could go forward. It did so, however, with reservations, which were expressed in Commissioner Blum's letter to HEW Associate Commissioner Van Lare of January 16, 1979, transmitting the necessary forms, assuring compliance with HEW regulations on protection of "human subjects."

> The Board's decision was based on a strict interpretation of HEW regulations concerning the protection of human subjects, which states that subjects are at risk if they are involved in activities which are not normal procedure and practice. The use of two-party vendor restricted payments is considered an accepted practice based upon federal and state law and regulations.
>
> The Board expressed serious reservations about the policy of vendor restricted payments and believes that its application, without proper implementation, can be harmful to public assistance recipients. But since the policy is accepted practice, the Board had no alternative but to rule that the project would not place subjects at risk.

The review board, of course, went far beyond its jurisdiction in commenting on current policy with respect to the use of the two-party checks.

HEW Considers the Proposal: November 1978–
February 1979

We must now go back slightly in time to November 1978, when
we began to hear from HEW regarding its official views of the revised
proposal submitted in late October. Both state and city officials involved in the project had kept in close touch with HEW officials at all
stages of its development and tried to accommodate their views to the
extent possible. But now it was HEW's turn for an official go at the
proposal.

The atmosphere for negotiations was not improved by a memorandum from Cesar Perales, Principal Regional Official of HEW, Region II, to Barry Van Lare, dated November 15, which was reported in
the *New York Times*. It indicated that Mr. Perales had met with Henry
Freedman and representatives of the Downtown Welfare Advocate
Center who strongly urged that HEW not grant the waiver requested
and offered Mr. Perales's personal opinion that "the procedure for tenant participation is not sensitive to the rights of welfare recipients."
He also indicated "serious misgivings about the efficacy of the entire
project," wondering "whether we know enough to make any judgment about it." Mr. Perales concluded by saying, "I am not satisfied
with the proposed plan and intend to formulate a plan that should be
more effective and that may begin to have a real impact on the housing stock in New York City." Another one of the critics of the project
who promised a better plan and has not yet produced one.

Mayor Koch felt it was necessary to increase public understanding of the proposal and held a press conference on December 5, 1978,
attended by some of the state and local officials from the Bronx areas
involved. In his statement, Mayor Koch reviewed the four linked factors on which the proposal was based:

Building abandonment in New York City is increasing at an
alarming rate.

More than $500 million of public funds goes toward shelter for
welfare recipients.

Unfortunately, some welfare recipients do not pay their rent and
have no justification for not doing so.

A program to require welfare clients to pay their rent in return
for improved building maintenance will benefit tenants and
owners alike.

The mayor added that federal law and regulations relating to the ceiling on two-party checks have served to exacerbate housing problems in New York and went on to say:

> And, to add insult to injury, a regional HEW official has just suggested that the City's demonstration proposal not be approved even though he has formulated no alternative solution and objects to the City's proposal on the vague grounds that it "is not sensitive to the rights of welfare recipients." In fact, this proposal safeguards the rights of clients to decent, safe housing by ensuring a reliable flow of revenue into their buildings.
>
> There can be no question that part—although by no means all—of the City's housing crisis is due to an inadequate flow of revenue into the older housing stock of this City.

Despite the mayor's efforts, we were to face from HEW more months of questions, many of which had already been answered in the project proposal and in exchanges with state officials. For example, what are present policies of HPD and HRA relating to the problem addressed by the proposed demonstration project, and do they contribute to the problem by encouraging clients to move to avoid paying rent arrears? What alternatives to two-party checks are available to alleviate housing problems? Could a smaller project—even a few buildings—adequately serve demonstration purposes? Concern was again expressed as to how we would evaluate the project, whether we could establish a control group, and whether we could identify separately all the factors that might lead to the success or failure of the demonstration to improve housing.

At a meeting with HEW officials in December 1978, attended by representatives of New York Senators Moynihan and Jacob Javits and Congressmen Bingham and Rangel, we again explained that we had no alternative to the use of the two-party check and that, to our knowledge, no one else in or outside the meeting room had one. While we could not guarantee success, this approach clearly had possibilities and should be tried as it imposed no serious hardship on the welfare recipients who participated and could help them. Finally, we strongly rejected the suggestion of one HEW official that it would be a disaster if the project were successful because that would justify the extension of the use of the two-party check for rent to all welfare clients.

On January 25, 1979, Barry Van Lare wrote of several more HEW concerns that needed to be resolved. The first related to an issue that had been a bone of contention from the beginning—that is, the involuntary participation of recipients who had a six-month record of regular rent payments but who failed to respond to the notices sent them. Although we felt it would substantially weaken the project's chances of success, we finally gave up on this objection in order to avoid the risk of HEW disapproving the project. It was agreed if such tenants mismanaged their rent grants after the project began, they would be placed on two-party checks, as under current procedures. Such procedures, of course, involve the usual delays and interruption of cash flow to landlords and would have weakened the inducement we hoped to offer them in order to obtain their written agreement for repairs and service maintenance.

We also agreed to expand the site office staff with personnel trained in welfare application procedures and eligibility determination for emergency assistance to satisfy the concern that clients might have problems if they could not use the rent money to meet some emergency situation.

Associate Commissioner Van Lare asked us again to develop a more specific list of objective criteria for determining which buildings would be permitted to participate in the project. We had already set forth ten criteria to state officials, and we stood on those but agreed that in the evaluation, we would, for example, relate degree of success or failure to a building's characteristics, concentration of welfare tenants, cost of removing violations, and the ratio of a building's income to expenses. Further, we presented a detailed evaluation plan to measure on a "before-after" basis the effects of two-party checks on housing service delivery and on the incidence of welfare tenant hardship resulting from an inability to use the two-party rent check for other purchases. Finally, we listed the criteria for gauging the degree of success of the project and indicated the result would determine the nature of the extension of the approach in other areas of New York City.

With this response, which was transmitted to HEW on February 25, 1979, we thought we had met all of the HEW requests for amendments and awaited a decision regarding the waiver by the end of March or early April 1979. This period would allow the usual six weeks to two months for completion of the HEW review process, including thirty days for review and comment by the Center on Social Welfare Policy and Law.

A Digression—Other Developments Regarding Two-Party Checks

At this point, I must digress to discuss other developments with respect to regulations regarding two-party checks, which were not part of the project but which might have had a direct impact on it. In November 1978, Barry Van Lare advised the HEW Regional Commissioner for Family Assistance in New York City that the city's procedures for instituting two-party checks on the basis of a landlord's written statement that the client had not paid rent for *one* month or more were invalid. "Rather, the full facts of the individual situation must be considered in order to provide a basis for an adequate demonstration of the recipients inability to manage funds."

This information was transmitted to NYSDSS, which immediately undertook a revision of its regulations and issued a draft that would permit a client to accumulate *two* or more months of arrears before HRA staff could consider a written request from the landlord for a two-party check. Further, the landlord would have to produce "evidence" that he attempted to collect the overdue rent, but it was not clear from NYSDSS's draft whether this evidence could simply be a letter from the landlord to the client or had to be an official dispossess notice. Even in the event of a two-month delinquency in rent payment, HRA could not put the client on restricted rent payments until the agency had notified the client, giving him or her ten days to request a conference with Income Maintenance (IM) center staff or an administrative review.

Under current regulations, HRA can immediately place the client on a restricted check after one month's delinquency, notify the client of the action and the reasons for it, and give him or her the opportunity to come to the IM center to explain if there was good cause—either the rent had been paid or there was a dispute over service or repairs. In the former event, the restriction is removed; in the latter, the client does not have to turn over the check to the landlord and can seek remedy with code enforcement agencies. In the meantime, the rent money is conserved.

Clearly, while the proposed change to permit a two-month rent arrears before HRA could take action gave more protection to the client, it also increased from six to eight weeks to three months or more the period before the landlord could obtain any remedy. Put another way, the current regulation tries to stop the hemorrhaging right away and then reviews the situation to determine the cause; if the restriction is not justified, it can be removed before the next welfare check is issued. The proposed regulation would permit this hemorrhaging to continue while HRA examined the situation to see if the client had good cause. As soon as we received the new draft regulations in January 1979, I advised Mayor Koch of this development, pointing out its general effect and its impact on the project and he immediately wrote to Robert Morgado protesting the new regulation.

The lineup of forces on the proposed changes in the state regulations was similar to the lineup on the Bronx demonstration project. They were hailed by the Center on Social Welfare Policy and Law, other welfare advocates, and City Council President Carol Bellamy, who said, "The proposed regulations will provide needed protection against the issuance of restricted rent checks to landlords who do not provide required services."

Groups concerned with housing for low-income families opposed the changes. For example, Harold Baer and Reginald Johnson, board chairman and president of the Settlement Housing Fund, a nonprofit sponsor and owner of 540 rehabilitated units of low- and moderate-income housing, wrote to NYSDSS: "Our experiences with non-rent paying public assistance recipients have demonstrated conclusively to us that *prompt payment* of rent is essential to the economic viability and social stability of housing for *all* people living in our developments."

As discussion with state officials proceeded in the effort to clarify HRA's current procedures so that they were clearly understandable to clients, HEW, in March 1979, issued *its* proposed new regulations, which, among other matters, would have prohibited the issuance of restricted checks based "solely on the fact that bills are not paid on a timely basis." HEW justified this provision on the ground that restricted or protective payments were not intended to deprive families of their ability to make choices in how they spend this money and did not permit such payments in cases where an assistance family's monthly expenses exceeds its income and therefore the family does not pay its rent.

At a meeting in Washington on April 10, 1979, with Barry Van Lare and other HEW officials in which NYSDSS and HRA representatives were joined by John Dempsey, Michigan Commissioner of Welfare, we strongly argued against HEW's proposal. A subsequent letter to HEW from Stanley Brezenoff, who succeeded me as commissioner of HRA, stated that congressional intent was clear and quoted, among others, Congressman Charles Rangel, who said during the House debate in support of the proposal to raise the ceiling on vendor-restricted payments:

> The cost of living has escalated significantly in the past few years, yet all too often because of financial pressures on government the benefits have not kept pace with costs. Under those circumstances, it is not incomprehensible that welfare recipients will find themselves faced with the hard choice of whether to meet their rent or to pay other pressing bills. When they fail to meet their rent obligations, it is left to local government to pick up the tab with no Federal or State reimbursement. This diverts funds from other social service programs and in so doing cripples programs designed to meet the needs of the underprivileged.

Commissioner Brezenoff further argued that delayed payment or nonpayment of rent raised the threat of eviction which placed children in jeopardy of being without shelter, and he pointed out that the procedures HRA had in place protected children and reflected congressional intent and language.

Of course, both the proposed state and federal regulations would have adversely affected the Bronx demonstration project. They would have prevented the assurance of a reasonable cash flow to the landlord in exchange for his agreement on repairs and services—which brings us back to the continuing negotiations with HEW on the demonstration project.

HEW Considers the Proposal—Some More: March–September 1979

As I indicated above, we anticipated a decision on the Bronx demonstration project from HEW by the end of March 1979. In early April, I called Associate Commissioner Van Lare, who said he thought we would have the decision in about a week. Instead, he called for *another* meeting with state and HRA officials, which was held on April 19 to discuss some additional issues.

As a result of this meeting, HRA added a new provision to the proposal to clarify the procedures to be followed in the event of a client's mismanagement of funds. It maintained current HRA practice of restricting funds when a family's mismanagement, which includes nonpayment of rent, places children in jeopardy. But HRA agreed to amend the notice to clients to inform them clearly that staff was available to discuss their situation and to reverse the decision in the situations already laid out in current procedures; these included instances in which rent had been used to cover a need that could be met by an emergency payment under current state regulations. Further, HRA would institute a review of the decision to impose the two-party check at the end of three months instead of the usual six months.

Finally, a compromise was reached on the evaluation approach to include not only the "before-after" analysis already embodied in the final proposal submitted in February but also a control group in at least one Community Planning District with characteristics as similar to those of Bronx CPDs 5 and 7 as was feasible; this control district would include a sample of buildings equal in number and similar in character to those participating in the demonstration. The control buildings would be subject only to the regular code enforcement activities administered by HPD.

In sum, HEW obtained the major points it had long wanted—no involuntary participation of clients unless there was a history of mismanagement in the six months preceding the beginning of the program; detailed procedures with respect to notices to clients; detailed procedures in maintaining the agreements with the landlords; and a detailed research and evaluation plan, including a control group. In addition, in response to the earlier request of NYSDSS, provision was made for regular inspection of buildings enrolled in the project every three months instead of six, as well as ad hoc inspections on the basis of tenant complaints. These modifications were formalized in an addendum to the proposal submitted to HEW in mid-May 1979.

Was HRA to be notified shortly of HEW's decision? Not exactly. In its revised form, the proposal had to be resubmitted to the Center on Social Welfare Policy and Law. HEW promised HRA a decision in about a month, that is, about the middle or end of June 1979. Commissioner Brezenoff advised Mayor Koch on July 10 that a favorable decision was expected about the second week of July. The month passed with no word from Washington, but by early August, HRA officials were led to understand that a letter granting the necessary waiver was ready for HEW Secretary Califano's approval. Before he signed it, however, President Carter announced several cabinet changes—including the replacement of Califano by Patricia Harris.

Califano's staff assigned to work with Secretary-Designate Harris's staff on the transition, in accordance with Califano's general instructions, decided that, in view of the controversy that had surrounded the proposal, he should not approve the project without offering Secretary-Designate Harris the choice of considering the matter. Her staff requested that it be left for her decision. After she officially took over, Mayor Koch lost no time in writing to Secretary Harris urging that she approve the proposal. Neither did the opponents lose any time. A letter to Secretary Harris prepared by the Center on Social Welfare Policy and Law and cosigned by representatives of the Community Council of Greater New York, the NAACP, the Metropolitan Council on Housing, the New York City chapter of the National Association of Social Workers, and the Downtown Welfare Advocate Center urged her to deny approval.[6] City Council President Bellamy also wrote to Secretary Harris, on August 17, urging her to disapprove the project or at least postpone a decision until Council President Bellamy had completed a research study she had undertaken some months earlier.*

In another letter to Secretary Harris, dated August 24, Mayor Koch referred to their telephone conversation that morning with respect to the project: "Joe Califano had agreed to it, and now you tell me you are rejecting it. I await your letter setting forth the reasons for your rejection."

Secretary Harris did not write but on September 5, NYSDSS was advised by HEW as follows:

> After many hours of study, Secretary Harris has decided not to approve the project on the basis of a number of serious concerns. In general, the research design of the proposal would make it impossible for the demonstration to meet its stated goals. For example, the hypothesis of the project could neither be verified nor denied because of the lack of a con-

---

*City Council President Carol Bellamy's study was issued at a press conference she held on November 11, 1979. I do not wish to comment on the study in detail except to say I share the criticisms of it made in the six-page letter, dated November 9, 1979, HRA Commissioner Stanley Brezenoff sent Council President Bellamy on behalf of himself and Anthony Gliedman, commissioner of HPD.

trol group of nonwelfare tenants, the probability that landlords who voluntarily participate would not be a
representative group, and the difficulty of distinguishing the
effects of the two-party check mechanism from the effects of
other initiatives (such as more frequent inspection).

Beyond research design questions, it seems unlikely
that the two-party rent check approach would represent
either an efficient income maintenance system for AFDC recipients or a significant improvement for landlords. At the
same time, the Secretary recognizes that the goals of the
proposed demonstration are worthy. HEW and HUD staff
are willing to work cooperatively with your department to
develop alternative approaches to achieve these goals in a
mutually agreeable fashion.

I am not privy to Mayor Koch's language when this communica-
tion was brought to his attention. In my own language, I must find
the letter of denial incredible. It is the first time the idea of a control
group of *nonwelfare tenants* was brought up. Further, I am not sure
what a representative group of landlords would be, but I assume that
it would have to include those "bad," "not to be trusted" landlords
who are milking the buildings they temporarily own and who haven't
any intention of providing required services to tenants. But all of us
always knew these landlords would not want to join the project and
that we would not have wanted them. We did want to work with the
many landlords who are struggling to retain their properties but cannot do so without an adequate cash flow and reasonable profitability.

As to the problem of distinguishing between the effects of the
two-party check and more frequent inspections, this is really Catch-
22. First, NYSDSS and HEW said we had to provide for more frequent
inspections to ensure that landlords were living up to their agreements
to justify putting clients on restricted checks. Then, HEW said it would
not be able to distinguish the effect of one from the other. Our whole
point was that one could not achieve much from inspections if the
landlords were not obtaining the rents due them and that both were
necessary to attempt to provide adequate housing for welfare clients.
Credulity is further strained by HEW's conclusion that the project
"seems unlikely" to work either for clients or landlords and, therefore,
it should not be tried.

Conclusion

The general public, which may express itself through polls on major issues or proposed legislation, is basically unaware of individual proposals for demonstration projects and cannot express itself pro or con. Indeed, most proposals to HEW requesting either funding or a waiver of a regulation would be reviewed only by HEW staff, a selected review committee of experts, and, in this case, the National Welfare Rights Organization or, rather, its surrogate, the Center on Social Welfare Policy and Law. The proposal for the Bronx demonstration project elicited a great deal of "public" comment but largely from special interest groups.

The workings of the democratic process frequently involve tensions and differing views among elected or appointed officials at the federal, state, and local levels of government. Further, various interest groups try to influence the outcome of legislative debate or executive administrative action. The outcome on any particular matter, in the nature of things, is never satisfactory to everyone. One hopes, however, that the outcome is generally satisfactory to the majority. Currents in American political life evident during recent years, specifically the proliferation of special interest groups, whether of the right or the left, conservative or liberal, in a period of declining voter participation, raise serious concerns about the effectiveness of the democratic process in achieving decisions satisfactory to the majority on a variety of issues that are important, though not of such overwhelming importance as to engage the attention of the general public.

The proposed demonstration had the support of most of the elected officials from the Bronx areas, of the three major newspapers in the city, and of the major organizations concerned with housing for low-income families. But it did not get the support of the welfare advocacy groups and the social welfare organizations; this coalition prevailed.

It is fair to ask why. Were the criteria HEW used to evaluate this project the same as the department applies to other demonstration projects submitted to it? Anyone acquainted with many of the demonstrations approved by HEW over the years would be inclined to answer in the negative.

The principle of money management, that is, the right of the welfare client to spend the grant as he or she wishes, was adopted in the original Social Security Act in 1935. It was an appropriate reaction at that time to the frequent abuses of the voucher system for food or clothing as it was implemented in many local welfare programs during the Great Depression—the client was sometimes limited to particular stores or was overcharged for the merchandise received.

But to regard the principle of money management as untouchable forever and in all situations is an act of faith and not an objective evaluation of the current situation in major urban areas in the country. And to refuse to permit a test of an approach to improving housing, which made a *prima facie* case of feasibility, is unscientific, to say the least. It was an experiment that, at worst, would have failed and drifted into social science oblivion, as have other experiments that have been tried. At best, we would have found an effective approach, though not necessarily the only one, to some improvement in housing for welfare clients. And during the experiment what dreadful burden would we have put on the welfare client? We would have required that the welfare grant for rent be used for rent and would have stood ready, as provided for under federal and state regulations, to meet emergency needs that might have arisen as a result of the use of the two-party check.

State and federal officials have their responsibilities and obligations. Certainly, these officials must ensure that a proposal, such as the Bronx demonstration project, is feasible and provides adequate protection to welfare clients. We adopted many of their suggestions, which served to strengthen the proposal substantially. But one cannot escape the conclusion that the decision to reject was a political decision, not reflective of the objective situation but only of political pressures from one bloc of special interest groups.

Where are we now? After one year of review, discussions, negotiations, compromises, and agreement, we are back to square one. HEW and HUD representatives came to New York City on September 28, 1979, to visit CPDs 5 and 7 for the first time and to begin discussions to develop mutually agreeable alternative approaches. As this article went to press in mid-December, no further word had been heard from HEW officials, and no further meetings have been held or even scheduled.

We had hoped to implement the demonstration in October 1978. It is now December 1979. In the meantime, what has been happening in Bronx CPDs 5 and 7? According to unpublished information available to HPD, thirty-seven buildings in CPD 5 were vacated between January 1 and October 31, 1979, just under one per week. These thirty-seven buildings included 1,379 rental units and housed more than 4,000 persons. Complaints of inadequate services and lack of repairs continue unabated, as does the parade of welfare clients brought into the Bronx Housing Court for nonpayment of rent.

A reiterated theme in many letters Mayor Koch and I wrote to state and federal officials was the necessity for early implementation of the project so housing services for welfare clients in the demonstration areas could be improved during the winter of 1978–1979. It did not happen. It looks as if nothing will be done in time to improve conditions in the winter of 1979–1980, either.

EPILOGUE: SUBSEQUENT EVENTS, 1980–1981

The sad tale told in the article "An Effort to Improve Welfare Housing—and What Happened to It" ended as 1979 drew to a close. Has anything more cheerful happened in the two years since then? The main outlines of subsequent developments can be sketched and they are instructive.

Efforts continued through much of 1980 to develop a substitute proposal, one which would avoid recourse to the use of the restricted, or two-party, check for the rent portion of the welfare grant; clearly HEW (now Health and Human Services—HHS) would not accept any proposal involving the two-party check. One plan, modest in scope, developed by HRA and HPD officials, proposed to establish a "rent assurance fund." Cooperating landlords could draw from the fund if a welfare client was in arrears in rent payments. If the client subsequently paid his rent, the landlord would return the sum to the fund; if the client did not, the fund would bear the loss. It was hoped that the plan could be financed from money available to the city from Community Development grants or other sources. The mayor was sympathetic to the proposal and efforts were made by his office to latch on to some funds but without immediate success.

While the rent assurance plan was still under consideration, Edward Logue, President of the South Bronx Development Corporation turned his attention to the problem and spurred another effort to develop a proposal. He enlisted the aid of Richard Nathan, Director, of the Urban Affairs Institute at Princeton University, and of the Vera

Institute, one of the major research organizations in New York. A rather elaborate plan was drafted involving the use of substantial federal funds to assist in the repair and rehabilitation of buildings in CPD's 5 and 7 which appeared to be salvageable. The plan was discussed with HHS officials, who appeared to be interested, but no commitment of federal funds was made. Time passed and nothing came of either plan.

By the fall of 1980, interest in CPD's 5 and 7 waned and efforts to improve housing for welfare clients in these areas ceased. Both of the plans developed required additional funding either from federal grants already allocated to the city or from new federal grants. The funding simply was not forthcoming. The experience confirms the view implicit in the original proposal that the major, if not the only, available source of funding for the improvement of welfare clients' housing is the portion of the welfare grant allocated for rent. If steps are not taken to ensure the payment of rent, welfare housing will deteriorate. Abandonment of buildings continued apace in CPD's 5 and 7, and the Bronx Housing Court suffered no lack of new cases brought in for nonpayment of rent.

Toward the end of 1981, a grassroots effort began to develop in CPD 5 started by the Community Development Board in cooperation with HPD's Neighborhood Preservation Office and HRA representatives in the human services cabinet (that is, representatives of various city agencies) in the district and the South Bronx Development Corporation office. Among its elements are HPD offers to help landlords secure loans for necessary repairs, HRA outreach to tenants to deal with their problems, and general efforts to secure the cooperation of landlords and tenants in improving building maintenance. It is a modest effort (as of the beginning of February 1982, five buildings had been signed up in the campaign) and will move only slowly. Though worthy in purpose, the area may be too far gone for it to prove of much help.

In the section of the original article entitled—"A Digression— Other Developments Regarding Two-Party Checks", I described new HEW draft regulations issued in March 1979 which would have imposed additional restrictions on the issuance of two-party checks in the event of nonpayment of rent and the opposition to them expressed by state and city officials in New York as well as by John Dempsey, Michigan Commissioner of Welfare.

Our pleas were in vain. The new regulations were issued March 28, 1980. Not only do they make it more difficult and time-consuming to place clients who did not pay their rent on two-party checks, they led to decisions in two court cases which made the situation worse. In *Montes v. Brezenoff, Blum in the U.S. District Court for the Southern District of New York,* the plaintiffs challenged the continuation of the use of restricted checks for the 26,000 cases placed under the restriction under the previous regulations. The court decision ordered HRA to remove the two-party rent check designation for these cases on the grounds that they had not been afforded the protection ordered by the new regulations. Since no appeal was taken, HRA had no choice but to comply. In *Gittler v. Blum, Krauskopf* litigated in the same court in 1981, the right of HRA to withhold the rent portion of the welfare grant from the client who does not pay his rent due to a dispute with the landlord over the services being provided came under challenge. The Regional Office of HHS advised NYSDSS that the challenged practice was in fact a restriction which could not be implemented without a finding of mismanagement and, further, that client withholding of rent in a dispute was not mismanagement. NYSDSS conceded on the issue and gave instructions in December 1981 to the local welfare agencies to cease reducing the welfare grant in such cases.

Mayor Koch has not lost interest in the problem. He wrote to HHS Secretary Richard Schweiker on June 5, 1981, describing the adverse effects of the March 1980 regulations on the housing situation in New York City. He pointed out that the city had been forced to take title to 11,000 buildings because of their abandonment by landlords. In describing the impact of the regulations on both private and public housing, he noted that delinquency in rent payments among N.Y.C. Housing Authority tenants was four times greater among tenants on welfare than among other tenants and that the delinquency rate among welfare tenants had tripled over the past several years. He urged Secretary Schweiker to consider amending the March 1980 regulations and to revert basically to the prior rules which provided adequate protection to AFDC clients.

And now begins a curious episode in the light of the Reagan administration stance on regulations in general, welfare administration in particular, and the removal, at its recommendation, of the 20 percent restriction on the issuance of vendor restricted checks to AFDC clients in the Budget Reconciliation Act of July 1981. There is now no restriction on the percentage of AFDC clients who can be placed on two-party checks in the event of mismanagement of their grants. Further, clients can now voluntarily request the restricted check, in the absence of past mismanagement, as an aid in avoiding future problems.

No reply to his June letter having been received, the Mayor wrote Schweiker again in early August, again urging reconsideration of the March 1980 regulations, with their cumbersome, time consuming procedures. It was clear that unless the regulations were changed, the removal of the 20 percent restriction in the law was of little use. The Secretary did reply to the Mayor on September 23, indicating the regulations were being revised but only to reflect the removal of the 20 percent limitation and the additional provision which allows restricted payments to be issued at the recipient's request; any further possible revisions were to be left to some future time with no indication whether this future time would be sooner or later.

Three months later, on December 24, the Mayor wrote to the Secretary pointing out that the limited changes in the regulations issued in September 1981 did nothing to improve the effectiveness of the process or to reduce the time necessary to impose a restricted payment on a client. Secretary Schweiker did reply promptly to the Mayor's third plea, advising him in a letter dated January 7, 1982, that the request would be handled expeditiously. That is where the matter stood as of early February 1982.

In the meantime, delinquent rent payments are as great a problem as ever. In the second quarter of 1981, HRA had to issue 17,672 special needs grants mainly to avoid dispossesses of clients who had not paid their rent out of their regular welfare grants, an increase of 59 percent over the previous year.[7] As indicated, the restrictions on all 26,000 AFDC recipients on two-party checks for rent because of previous delinquency in rent payments were removed in March 1981 as a result of a court order. Since then the numbers have gradually built up as new cases of default of rent payments occur for two months or more, and after review of the case, a finding of mismanagement is reached. As of November 1981 approximately 12,800 cases were receiving restricted checks for rent. But clearly this is substantially below the number who are delinquent in rent payments.

The housing situation of welfare clients in New York has not improved in this winter of 1981–1982.

NOTES

Chapter 1

[1] One of my studies indicated that in about 20 percent of AFDC cases, the mother chose the welfare option over maintaining or forming an intact family. Others disagree. See Blanche Bernstein and William Meezan, *Impact of Welfare on Family Stability*.

[2] These data were obtained in a series of studies done in 1972–1975 by the Research Department, Center for New York City Affairs, New School for Social Research, under my direction.

[3] Robert B. Hill, "Black Families in the 70's: The State of Black America 1980," quoted by Daniel Patrick Moynihan in "Children and Welfare Reform," *Journal of the Institute for Socio-Economic Studies* 6 (Spring 1981): 10.

[4] Martin Anderson, *The Political Economy of Welfare Reform in the United States* (Palo Alto, Calif.: Hoover Institute, Stanford University, 1978), p. 164.

[5] The attempt to set up this demonstration project is fully described in Blanche Bernstein, "An Effort to Improve Welfare Housing—and What Happened to It," *City Almanac* (October 1979): 1–15. This article is included with an epilogue in the appendix to this book, as a case study in the politics of welfare.

Chapter 2

[1]Data obtained through the good offices of Marlene Vidibor, New York Regional Office of Family Assistance, Department of Health and Human Services, from special tabulations prepared by the Washington office. These tabulations separated the usual published data for the total AFDC caseload into AFDC and AFDC-U.

[2]Ibid.

[3]Charles R. Morris, *The Cost of Good Intentions: New York City and the Liberal Experience* (New York: Norton, 1980), p. 70.

[4]Ibid., p. 69.

[5]Blanche Bernstein, "Welfare in New York City" in the *City Almanac* (4), no. 5. (New York: Center for New York City Affairs, New School for Social Research, February 1970), p. 10.

[6]Blanche Bernstein, *Welfare and Income in New York City* (New York: Center for New York City Affairs, New School for Social Research, August 1971), pp. 18–26.

[7]The Scott Commission Task Force on Social Services said in its report, *Social Services in New York City* (March 1973), that it believed the pilot tests were successful and that it saw "no valid reason for delay" (p. 36). It estimated the loss as in excess of $100 million per year.

[8]*Marital and Family Characteristics of the Labor Force, March 1979*, Special Labor Force Report 237. (Washington, D.C.: U.S. Department of Labor, January 1981), table 4, p. 50.

[9]See, for example, Blanche Bernstein, Michael Rowan, and Anne Shkuda, *Obstacles to Employment of Employable Welfare Recipients* (New York: Center for New York City Affairs, New School for Social Research, June 1974), p. 61.

[10]Discussion between Samuel Ehrenhalt and author.

[11]Eli Ginzberg, "Employment Goals as Reality in Public Welfare," *Journal of the American Public Welfare Association*, 36, no. 2 (Spring 1978):31.

[12]Data obtained by telephone from Al Peden, Congressional Budget Office, August 13, 1981. These estimates differ to some extent from the Executive Office estimates. However, neither CBO nor the Executive Office assumes any savings from the work programs in fiscal 1982. Excluded from the tabulation are estimated savings of $16 million from a reduction in the federal match for staff training from 75 to 50 percent and savings in administrative costs of $11 million. These items do not affect benefits to welfare clients. The estimate of zero savings from eliminating the limit of 20 percent on vendor-restricted checks is misleading, as it is based on the assumption that the federal government does not now bear the cost of duplicate checks issued to cover unpaid rent or

electric bills and not fully recovered from the client. Such an assumption underestimates the accounting skills available in the local welfare agencies to enhance the federal contribution. In any event, the states and localities will certainly obtain some significant savings from prompt use of the vendor-restricted, or two-party, check to prevent the accumulation of unpaid rent and electricity bills.

Chapter 3

[1] New York State, Department of Social Services, Office of Child Enforcement, *Report to the Governor, 1977.*

[2] U.S., Congress, Senate, Committee on Finance, (Washington, D.C.: Government Printing Office, 1975), p. 3.

[3] Blanche Bernstein to Georgia McMurray, chairperson, Parent Locator and Support Monitoring Committee, Community Council of Greater New York, March 7, 1978. This letter was included in *Who Should Support the Children?.*

[4] A report in the *New York Times* on July 21, 1981, one of a special series on children, stated that 711,742 cases of child abuse were reported in the country as a whole in 1980; this figure is the equivalent of 1.1 percent of the total population under eighteen of 61.7 million. Even if actual cases are triple those reported, the figure would come to 3.3 percent. And, as noted, most child abuse is committed by parents in the home.

[5] Blanche Bernstein and William Meezan, *The Impact of Welfare on Family Stability* (New York: Center for New York City Affairs, New School for Social Research, June 1975), p. 30.

[6] U.S. Department of Labor, Bureau of Labor Statistics, *Employment and Earnings* (Washington, D.C., December 1981), table A35, p. 31. Data are not available for Hispanic adult males. Their unemployment rate may be somewhat higher than for black males.

[7] David L. Chambers, *Making Fathers Pay: The Enforcement of Child Support* (Chicago: University of Chicago Press, 1979).

[8] Ibid., p. 39.

[9] Data obtained from the Bureau of Child Support, Human Resources Administration.

[10] U.S., Department of Health and Human Services, Office of Child Support Enforcement, *Child Support Enforcement Statistics* (Washington, D.C., May 1981), table 14.

[11] U.S., Department of Health and Human Services, Office of Child Support Enforcement, *Child Support Report* 3, no. 4 (April 1981): 7.

[12] U.S., Department of Health and Human Services, Office of Child Sup-

port Enforcement, *Child Support Report* 3, no. 6 (June 1981): 7. The New York City figure was obtained from tables made available by the Human Resources Administration, Bureau of Child Support. This figure, however, like the published figures for New York and the other states, does not include estimated savings from AFDC cases closed when efforts to locate the "absent" father result in finding him in the home with the mother and children, or from comparable savings in food stamps or Medicaid. Further, as a result of cooperative arrangements established between the Medicaid and child support programs, successful efforts are being made, effective May 1980, to offset Medicaid costs by utilizing the health insurance coverage which the responsible parent may have or be able to obtain.

Chapter 4

[1] The Library of Congress, Congressional Research Service, "Food Stamp Program Reform," mimeographed (Washington, D.C.: Issue Brief No. 1B77070, January 6, 1978), p. 1.

[2] See U.S. Congress, Senate, Hearings before the Committee on Government Operations, Subcommittee on Federal Spending Policies, Efficiency and Open Government, 94th Cong., 1st sess., April 28–29 and May 2, 1975; U.S., Congress, Senate, Hearings before the Committee on Agriculture, Subcommittee on Nutrition and Human Needs, 94th Cong., 1st sess., Fall 1975; U.S. Congress, House, Hearings before the Committee on Agriculture, 94th Cong., 2d sess., January–April 1976.

[3] Data obtained from Marjorie Rosen, Chief Statistician, Food and Nutrition Service, Mid-Atlantic region.

[4] U.S. Congress, House of Representatives, *A House Report on S1309 C,* Report No. 96-788, 96th Cong., 2 sess. Submitted by Congressman Foley of Washington for the Committee on Agriculture on February 27, 1980, pp. 95–96.

[5] Data obtained by phone from Roger Hitchner, Congressional Budget Office. Mr. Hitchner indicated that CBO's figures may vary somewhat from the executive branch estimates. Puerto Rico not included.

Chapter 5

[1] Otto Kerner et al. *Report of the National Advisory Commission on Civil Disorders* (New York, E. P. Dutton, Inc., 1968).

[2]Martin Anderson, *Welfare: The Political Economy of Welfare Reform in the United States* (Stanford, Calif.: Hoover Institution, Stanford University Press, 1978), p. 49.

[3]Moses Abramovitz, "Welfare Quandaries and Productivity Concerns," presidential address, American Economic Association, September 6, 1980. Reprinted from the *American Economic Review*, 71, no. 1 (March 1981).

[4]"Surfacing the Scratch," editorial commentary, *Barrons*, February 9, 1980, p. 7.

[5]Quoted in the *New York Times*, April 18, 1981, p. 1 and continuation.

[6]Anne Shkuda, *Former Welfare Families: Independence and Recurring Dependency* (New York: Center for New York City Affairs, New School for Social Research, 1976).

[7]Quoted in ibid., p. 86. From G. J. Duncan and J. N. Morgan, eds. *Five Thousand American Families—Patterns of Economic Progress* (Ann Arbor: Institute for Social Research, University of Michigan, 1976).

[8]Beverly L. Johnson, *Marital and Family Characteristics of the Labor Force, March 1979*, Special Labor Force Report 237 (Washington, D.C.: U.S. Department of Labor, January 1981), p. 50.

[9]Ibid., p. 49.

[10]James R. Hosek, *The AFDC-Unemployed Fathers Program and Welfare Reform*, HEW Publication R-2471 (Santa Monica, Calif.: Rand Corporation, August 1979).

[11]Gilbert Y. Steiner, *The Futility of Family Policy* (Washington, D.C.: Brookings Institution, 1981).

[12]Quoted in *Welfare Watch*, published by the New York Urban Coalition Resource Center, April 1981.

[13]See Martin Kilson, "Black Social Classes and Intergenerational Poverty," *Public Interest*, Summer 1981, especially pp. 72–75.

Appendix. A Case Study in the Politics of Welfare

[1]New York City Department of Housing Preservation and Development, Office of Program and Management Analysis (Bruce J. Gould, executive director), "Housing and the Public Assistance Tenant," draft prepared by Barbara Elstein (New York, September 1979).

[2]U.S., Bureau of the Census, *1978 New York City Housing and Vacancy Survey*, in Peter Marcuse, *Rental Housing in the City of New York: Supply and Condition 1975–1978* (New York, January 1979), p. 208.

[3]Data obtained from the U.S. Bureau of Labor Statistics' regional office in New York City indicate that real expendable earnings of production workers declined about 9 percent between 1972 and 1979 and 3 percent between 1974 and 1979.

[4]Thomas Appleby and Daniel L. Miller, "Welfare Shelter Payments Should Be Used to Stimulate Improvement in Housing Stock," *Journal of Housing*, published by the National Association of Housing and Redevelopment Officials, March 1979.

[5]James Dumpson and Mitchell Ginsberg are members of the task force. As indicated before, we consulted them at an early stage, and they appeared to approve the general design. But at the meeting when the task force considered it, Ginsberg joined in opposing the proposal; Dumpson was not present but apparently also opposed it.

[6]*Currents*, newsletter of the New York City chapter, National Association of Social Workers, 21m, no. 1 (October 1979).

[7]*New York City Social Report*, Office of Policy and Economic Research, N.Y.C. Human Resources Administration, November 1981. p. 15.

Index

211